Writing for Peer Reviewed Journals

C000172246

It's not easy getting published, but everyone has to do it. *Writing for Peer Reviewed Journals* presents an insider's perspective on the secret business of academic publishing, making explicit many of the dilemmas and struggles faced by all writers, but rarely discussed. Its unique approach is theorised *and* practical. It offers a set of moves for writing a journal article that is structured and doable but also attends to the identity issues that manifest on the page and in the politics of academic life.

The book comprehensively assists anyone concerned about getting published; whether they are early in their career or moving from a practice base into higher education or more experienced, but still feeling in need of further information. Avoiding a 'tips and tricks' approach, which tends to oversimplify what is at stake in getting published, the authors emphasise the production, nurture and sustainability of scholarship through writing – a focus on both the scholar and the text or what they call *text work/identity work*. The chapters are ordered to develop a systematic approach to the process, including such topics as:

- The writer
- The reader
- What's the contribution?
- Beginning work
- Refining the argument
- Engaging with reviewers and editors

Writing for Peer Reviewed Journals uses a wide range of multi-disciplinary examples from the writing workshops the authors have run in universities around the world: including the UK, Canada, Australia, New Zealand, Ireland, South Africa, Norway, Sweden, Denmark and the United States. This international approach coupled with theoretically grounded strategies to guide the authoring process ensure that people at all stages of their career are addressed. This lively book uses a combination of personal stories, student texts, published journal abstracts and excerpts from interviews with journal editors and publishers. Written in an accessible style, one which does not use the patronising 'you' of advice books, it offers a collegial approach to a task which is difficult for most scholars, regardless of their years of experience.

Pat Thomson is Professor of Education in the School of Education, University of Nottingham, UK.

Barbara Kamler is Emeritus Professor at Deakin University, Melbourne, Australia.

Writing for Peer Reviewed Journals

Strategies for getting published

Pat Thomson and
Barbara Kamler

Routledge
Taylor & Francis Group

LONDON AND NEW YORK

First published 2013
by Routledge
2 Park Square, Milton Park, Abingdon, Oxon OX14 4RN

Simultaneously published in the USA and Canada
by Routledge
711 Third Avenue, New York, NY 10017

Routledge is an imprint of the Taylor & Francis Group, an informa business

© 2013 P. Thomson and B. Kamler

The right of P. Thomson and B. Kamler to be identified as authors of this
work has been asserted by them in accordance with sections 77 and 78
of the Copyright, Designs and Patents Act 1988.

All rights reserved. No part of this book may be reprinted or reproduced
or utilised in any form or by any electronic, mechanical, or other means,
now known or hereafter invented, including photocopying and recording,
or in any information storage or retrieval system, without permission in
writing from the publishers.

Trademark notice: Product or corporate names may be trademarks or
registered trademarks, and are used only for identification and
explanation without intent to infringe.

British Library Cataloguing in Publication Data
A catalogue record for this book is available from the British Library

Library of Congress Cataloging in Publication Data
Thomson, Pat, 1948–
    Writing for peer reviewed journals: strategies for getting published /
Pat Thomson and Barbara Kamler.
        p. cm.
    1. Journalism–Authorship–Vocational guidance. 2. Peer review.
    3. Manuscript preparation (Authorship)–Handbooks, manuals, etc.
    4. Publishers and publishing.
    I. Kamler, Barbara. II. Title.
    PN147.T46 2013
    808.02–dc23   2012010077

ISBN: 978–0–415–80930–6 (hbk)
ISBN: 978–0–415–80931–3 (pbk)
ISBN: 978–0–203–09707–6 (ebk)

Typeset in Galliard
by Swales & Willis Ltd, Exeter, Devon
Printed and bound by CPI Group (UK) Ltd, Croydon, CR0 4YY

Contents

Illustrations

Figures

Tables

Abstracts

Acknowledgements

We want to acknowledge the ways in which the very many academics who have attended our workshops have shaped this book. We have worked all of our ideas over time in many different places with many different participants. We particularly want to thank those people who have donated their less-than-polished texts, both for our benefit and that of this book's readers. Their generosity makes this text possible and we hope that readers will approach the texts as unconditional gifts to the learning of others. We want to note, in particular, that we are grateful to the writers who have allowed us to use their abstracts and titles here and elsewhere. While we highlight the problems these individual writers face, in our experience these problems are widespread, although not widely discussed. We thus urge readers not to see these as inadequate texts, but works in progress. What is required is a new way of reading analytically to see what writing is and what it may become. We would hate to think that anyone might see these draft texts as emerging from the work of deficient scholars. No red markers please!

We have given all these writers pseudonyms. There are, however, some in the text who we call by their own name, with their permission. So, it's thanks particularly to Simon Bailey and Kerry Vincent for producing some writing about writing specifically for this book, and to the co-authors who graciously allowed us to interview them – Bob Lingard and Fazal Rizvi, Michelle Fine and Lois Weis and Michael Peters and Tina Besley.

We thank Wiley-Blackwell for permission to use a screen shot of the *British Journal of Clinical Pharmacology* 65 (3) 377–385, Graham Hobbs for his reasons why articles get rejected, and Taylor and Francis for their foresight in having provided us – and everyone else as well, since they are published on the Education Arena website – with 'horse's mouth' interviews with journal editors.

The first draft of this book was written in two very intensive eight-day blocks, the first in Singapore and the second in Melbourne. In between and after we also wrote, emailed and skyped. Our forgiving partners Randy and Greg have, as ever, been tolerant of our absentmindedness and obsessive discussion of yet another text. We are grateful for their continued support and indulgence.

Lastly, we would like to thank our publisher, the fabulous and always frolicsome Philip Mudd, whose friendship and perpetual enthusiasm have encouraged us to work not only on this text but also on a second edition of the companion volume on doctoral writing pedagogies – coming soon! To the rest of the team at Routledge, our thanks for their usual efficient support and service.

Introduction
Why this book now?

It's not as if we need another book on academic publishing. So why are we writing this one? There are now countless self-help texts for academics at every stage of their career. Most offer some useful advice and others have helpful examples and exercises. Very few are grounded in a sound theoretical framework which recognises and explains the complex tangle of identity work and text work shaped and limited by social, cultural, institutional and disciplinary practices. In this book we offer both a combination of theoretically grounded tools to think with *and* strategies to guide the authoring process. We provide an insider's perspective on the secret business of academic publication.

We have both spent a lot of time working with early career researchers, including doctoral researchers, in publication workshops. We've often been surprised, given how much emphasis is now placed on publishing, that many less experienced academics are ill-prepared for the challenges of academic writing. It seems that the number of years people spend reading other people's research, doing a research project and then writing the PhD doesn't equate to acquiring the know-how necessary to get into print.

In our workshops we see people who are stressed and distressed, working within performance-driven university systems. They are required to produce, but feel paralysed and terrorised. They send out articles, they receive criticism, they don't know how to deal with critique and they shelve their text, promising that they will get around to it some time. They don't tell people about the experience because they are ashamed, and because they don't know precisely what it is that they are expected to do. Another common scenario is that they write one article from their thesis that attempts to summarise all of its key features and are then so exhausted by the editing that is required that they lose heart and never try again. Some people write a research report but then never turn it into an academic text. Some, of course, never try at all and have to find a series of excuses for their department heads about why they haven't had time to write and how they are going to do it soon.

We have found that the vast majority of researchers are very good at reporting and describing a set of findings. They can tell you what they did, what they found, and what the research site looked like. They often have interesting anecdotes, observations and categorisations. But they lack the confidence to argue and package what they have to say in the kind of format and language that a journal will find acceptable. It is as if they are stuck in a kind of textual deep rut, where metaphorically spinning the wheels harder and faster will only dig them in deeper.

As we will show, the key to the journal article is not only having an argument, but also the stance to assert its significance. Some people call this confidence. We reject this. The common-sense understanding of confidence suggests that it is something acquired through experience. This is not helpful to tentative writers. It's as if the new researcher can only gain confidence from being published, but needs the confidence to get published in the first place. This is a paralysing catch-22. There *are* ways for researchers to break out of this conceptual trap. Getting published isn't an easy task, but it's not impossible. No matter how terrifying the prospect, there are strategies writers can use to produce a text that stands a reasonable chance of being well received.

In this book we offer a set of moves for writing a peer reviewed journal article. This is not a recipe, nor is it the only way to approach writing. But it is structured, practical and doable. It breaks up what looks like one task – writing the journal article – into a series of pieces. Other books on the market do this too. However, we offer a particular set of angles on the writing game, attending to the identity issues that inevitably manifest themselves on the page and in the politics of academic life.

If you were to eavesdrop on the workshops we conduct you would hear and see us moving around the room, gesticulating wildly, asking: So what? Who needs to know this? Who cares? Who wants to know about your research study? What does it have to offer? How is it like what others have done? What is new? Where is the innovation? Who will be interested outside the local context where you work? We don't ask these questions because we are cruel or difficult people, but because we know that if writers cannot answer these questions they cannot get published.

We create a safe environment where it is OK to ask these questions in public and allow people to struggle with them, even before they know what the answers might be. We cannot do this in a book. What we can do is frame our questions as exemplars and strategies which recreate some of the processes that we use, albeit without the interaction and our eccentricities.

It is usual for people who write these kinds of books to tell the reader how much experience they have, in order to make their advice credible. We won't do this for long. Check our websites if you need a detailed CV. We will tell you that we have, separately and together, run workshops in Australia, the UK, the US, Norway, Denmark, Canada, South Africa, Ireland, New Zealand and for AARE (Australian Association for Research in Education), AERA (American Educational Research Association), BERA (British Educational Research Association) and ECER (European Conference on Educational Research). We have worked in universities as teachers, supervisors and researchers. We sit on editorial boards, we edit journals, special issues of journals and books. Enough already. The point is we know 'the writing problem' from all sides. And we think there needs to be more talk about it, more public discussion of the less punitive kind. We hope that this book contributes to more openness and less embarrassed silences and no shame.

We imagine that the reader of this book is an early career writer, either post-PhD or close to finishing a PhD, not necessarily young in years, but relatively new to academic publication. Some readers will come from newer disciplines where there is an emerging tradition of academic writing, others will come from practice-based work settings where they are obligated to focus strongly on innovation and development. And of course, there will be readers from more established disciplines where there is already a strong journal culture, with escalating expectations about getting published in the most prestigious journals in the field. We attempt to address each of these situations in this book, because we have a sense that publishing careers and identities are ongoing and vary, depending on the specific contexts. There is also anxiety associated with context and career stage which we want to acknowledge and address.

The labour of writing

We want to say at the start of this book that writing is not easy. We often find it highly frustrating. We sometimes find ourselves, like Patrick Sullivan in the quotation below, confounded by the hard work of producing text.

> The other day while writing in my office there was a diffident tap on the door. I was startled and turned sharply. Anna, our admin assistant, was clearly concerned about me. 'Are you alright?' I realised I'd been slumped with my head in my hands trying to craft a particularly difficult sentence or two for a journal article with a deadline looming. It must have looked like emotional breakdown, but I'd only been caught in the act of writing. Writing is hard. If you are having trouble writing it is probably because it is hard, not because you are unusually dense. It is hard because it is an act of translation, not simply of the world into the word, but our thoughts about the ordering of the world. These need to be dragged from our heads onto the page. Some teachers take a very pragmatic, modernist approach

to research: gather your data, order your data, present your data, explain your data. The world isn't like that, and nor is human thought. You cannot know what you think until you have put it into words. Writing is thinking in the same way as thrashing your arms around is swimming. One is the material expression of the other.

(Sullivan, undated)

Patrick Sullivan elegantly sums up one of the most crucial things about writing. It is labour. It is headwork. It takes time as well as skill. But it is also highly emotionally charged work which can make us feel despair, anger, fear, satisfaction and great joy, depending on the stage of writing. When we think about the academic writing that we do, we often think in visual terms, trying to encapsulate the combination of intellectual, emotional and sometimes physical effort it takes. Maybe it is pulling teeth out very slowly, climbing a very slippery mountain or – on a good day – running to catch up with our ideas as they tumble out onto the page. Whatever the situation, we can be sure that it is about thinking *and* feeling as well.

Interviews with experienced writers show that they have very different approaches to the labour of writing. Some writers go into their study at an appointed time, usually in the early morning, and do not leave until they have written a particular number of words. This daily output has to be edited and worked on, and much of it may be abandoned. However, it is the production of writing every day that is most important. This is writing as regular work. Not all writers work in this way. Like Patrick Sullivan, they may sit for hours, read, garden or walk while they are percolating an idea and its textual representation. Some combine mornings churning out words with afternoons spent thinking and reading.

Whatever the approach, writing in general, and writing journal articles in particular, is a form of scholarly self-discipline. Foucauldians might see a daily writing routine as an act of self-creation via an ethic of the scholarly self. Writing most days can be seen as a practice of care which the scholar chooses in order to produce and maintain the ethic of 'professing' – speaking for knowledge and its (re)production and communication within a community of scholars. Just as Greek athletes spent time each day immersed in their personal training rituals (Foucault, 1978), scholars who spend regular time 'grooming' their scholarly writing selves are embodying scholarship, and disciplining themselves to the academic life.

Inevitably, we don't always feel like writing. It is hard work to push on if it's not easy and doesn't flow. But it's important, after we've stopped for a few days to go to a conference or attend the consistent round of meetings, to resume the writing routine as soon as we can.

Peter Elbow's (1973) classic text *Writing without teachers* offers spontaneous writing as a means of getting started on an article, and Robert Boice has written an entire book about how to get from generative writing (the process of developing ideas) to what he calls 'regular productivity'. His *Professors as writers: A self-help guide to productive writing* (Boice, 1990) could certainly be useful to those who want some assistance in finding a system for self-regulating their writing.

We are mostly of the write-a-given-number-of-words-a-day variety of scholars, but we do not advocate this as the only approach. It does, however, make sense for us and for many others with whom we work. It is not something that Barbara always did. She has, however, now adopted a 'just write' tactic rather than sitting with head-in-hands. We both leave head-in-hands for the refining stage of writing, the crafting, editing and revising.

Writing in performative times

There is increasing pressure on academics to write. Performative regimes (see Power, 1997, 2004; Strathern, 2000) in many countries now judge the worth of an academic by the number of their publications, or through some quasi-measure of quality such as download data or citations for the paper. Increasingly academics, regardless of their location, must also write in English. This is both contentious and sometimes extraordinarily difficult (Canagarajah, 2002). Tenure and promotion committees increasingly look at publications as *the* measure of quality, not simply one aspect of what it means to be a scholar. This pressure to publish can lead to people rushing into print well before the article is ready. Stephen Ball, himself widely and well published, notes:

> A lot of work is nothing more than re-inventing the wheel, the same idea coming round repeatedly. What gets lost in the rush to publish is a sense of accumulation, building on other things, developing and moving on. Most writing just stands on its own – 'I want to say this' – and too often the history of ideas, and concepts and analysis is ignored, in effect erased in the writing.
>
> (Carnell *et al.*, 2008: 71)

As well as the problem of premature publication and the push for the highest scoring journals and citations, there is also an increasingly competitive market for the limited number of postdoctoral awards and teaching positions. Pat has recently taken part in ranking applications for three-year postdoctoral awards in her own university: the top ranked candidate was five years out of the PhD and already had five books and numerous journal articles. The sheer quantity of this output was almost impossible for any other applicant to come near. This emergent cut-throat academic world is not one we wish to support and we are not writing this book simply to service these kinds of audit and competitive regimes.

We are committed to academic publishing that has something to contribute, not to league tables, but to scholarship as the production of knowledge. We know that we cannot turn our backs on research quality exercises, but that is not our prime interest.

Accordingly, readers will *not* find in this book discussions of how to get into the allegedly top journals. Rather, we focus on how to choose the best journals with the readership that will be interested in the publication being written. Nor will readers find extensive discussions of citation indices or the proliferation of academic journals, although we do briefly entertain these in Chapter 2. We take these things as inevitable and also contestable, but not central to our book's major ideas and strategies.

Our concerns about audit cultures, however, do make us *very* interested in what universities can do to contribute to writers and their writing, over and above counting them.

Writing as a way of scholarly life

Universities generally consist of numerous buildings, each of which has long corridors of closed doors. Behind each door is a solitary scholar beavering away, unless of course they are in a meeting. Our closed-door universities developed out of religious practices. The first universities were indeed very often initiatives of churches, and the direct lineage from monastic cells to academic offices is not hard to see.

But it is important not to get carried away with this version of history, and to remember that very few of the religious precursors to the modern university were grounded in practices of individual and isolated meditations and profound silences. Those precious illuminated manuscripts, now resplendent in our archives, were generally produced in very social settings; even if the cell was the site of production rather than a shared workroom, all of the artists knew that they were contributing to a common endeavour.

These days it is possible to see universities as more or less like silent meditations, more or less like groups working for social and mutual ends. In our view, the most enjoyable but also productive institutions are those where writing is a collective practice and a common endeavour. We are not alone in thinking this.

When asked about his writing practices, the linguist-turned-multimodal-design scholar Gunther Kress stressed the connection between the social discursive nature of writing and the critical role of the discipline and place where the writing occurs. When he was asked about what helped his writing he remarked:

> I couldn't think of writing separately from a whole much wider social environment. So what helped me in writing was moving through a place, specifically the University of East Anglia, a long time ago, where other people were writing, so it was a normal thing to do, it wasn't unusual . . . But then, specifically, having friends and colleagues with whom I was working who had confidence in the kinds of things I was thinking, and therefore having the confidence to put those things, which otherwise had been private and unusual and maybe strange and certainly not to be paraded in public, putting them down on paper as in publishing. It's that, it was about confidence in the community that allowed me then the confidence that people get from feedback, from people who I thought much of, who were friends and colleagues. That allowed me to take bearings . . . It was that really. So it's not writing as a mechanical or separate or decontextualised task or process.
>
> (Carnell *et al.*, 2008: 130–131)

Kress suggests that working in a supportive organisational culture was a crucial prior condition for his writing. He reinforces the role of others in creating the conditions necessary for gaining confidence as a writer. He harks back perhaps to the kind of religious order which was social and communally supportive; the ethos was of shared commitment and mutual endeavour.

There is, we suggest, a role for collective others in our individual and collaborative writing (we explore this idea further in Chapter 9). Developing these kinds of supportive writing cultures certainly requires leadership, but it also depends on the agency, initiative, choice and buy-in of communities of scholars. We have written about such cultures in relation to doctoral writing, but we note that much more might be investigated here and written about. There are some institutions which are much better at building writing cultures than others, and we need to know more about what they do.

Virtual support for writing

In recent times academic cultures have spread beyond material geographic location. Places of work are no longer confined to postcodes, but are distributed across time/space through terminals and screens. New approaches to developing writing cultures have emerged.

There is now a plethora of websites, blogs and tweets which offer writing advice. Indeed, Pat has a blog, *Patter*, on writing and research (http://www.patthomson.wordpress.com). Some of these websites are inevitably more helpful than others, as are the advice books on offer. And, just as with the books, there is little guidance available about which advice is good/bad (see Kamler and Thomson, 2008, for a critique of doctoral advice books).

But in addition to the advice that now proliferates, there are also new forms of support for writing, new virtual writing groups. For example, Charlotte Bunch, the originator of the PhD2published website (www.PhD2published.com) recently declared November 2011 #AcBoWriMo. She had observed the success of #NoBoWriMo – Novel and Book Writing Month – and decided that a similar venture – Academic Book Writing Month – should be tried. The idea spread around the world through a set of interlocking websites and tweet followers and each day more and more doctoral and early career researchers were sharing their daily word counts, strategies for overcoming writer's block and various tips and tricks they found on advice websites. #AcBoWriMo, and its ongoing sibling #acwri, is an indication of the potential of the virtual as a site for mutual support and endeavour. While it might not substitute for the kind of scholarly writing culture that Gunter Kress enjoyed, or the structure of writing groups or writing mates we discuss in Chapter 9, the web certainly offers possibilities for new ways of rethinking academic writing practices.

What's in this book?

Most of the books on writing for academic publishing offer a step-by-step approach: beginning with finding the journal, developing the text through drafting and redrafting, then submitting the article and revising it. While we do cover all of these topics, we have chosen not to organise the text as a set of stages where the writer moves simply, logically and smoothly from one to the next. This is misleading. Writing often happens in fits and bursts and goes backwards and forwards, round and round.

We are concerned to develop constructive strategies and there are many on offer throughout our text. Our point of difference with many of the advice books is that we are not interested in writing development per se. We are interested in the production, nurture and sustainability of scholarship. This concern with scholarship equates to a focus on both the scholar and the text, in their disciplinary and national and international contexts. We call this identity work/text work. We explain this framework in some detail in Chapter 1. For now it is sufficient to say that we highlight the kinds of work – the intellectual and emotional labour – involved in hatching an initial idea and then getting it to a fully-fledged text. We offer a theorised approach rather than a set of tips and tricks. Through the use of texts from writers across the spectrum of experience, we show the complexity of the scholarly endeavour, its difficulties and its sometimes pleasures/pains.

We take a pedagogical approach to academic writing. Our book has grown out of the work that we have done in workshops and courses. However, unlike our previous book, *Helping doctoral students write: Pedagogies for supervision* (Kamler and Thomson, 2006), this book is not intended to be used primarily in teaching or supervision settings. We imagine it as a text which early career scholars might use, singly and in writing groups, as a means of working on their own writing. In this sense, the book is profoundly pedagogical in that it subscribes to a view that learning is a process of becoming, made possible through intellectual interaction with resources/events/places/experiences. We have focused on what affordances we might make available through a book format. Readers will therefore not find a set of steps to follow, nor medical metaphors and remedial prescriptions. While appreciating the need to make the tasks of scholarship appear manageable, we do not want to underestimate its difficulties, nor indeed, its rewards. We have, therefore, organised the book around a set of issues which we have found to be key to making sense of the practices of scholarly writing and publishing.

Readers may want to read the text straight through. There is a logic to the order and the first three chapters do establish some key concepts used in the remainder of the book. However, each chapter does to some extent stand alone and writers who are already at a particular point in their writing may want to move to the relevant chapter straight away. To that end, it is helpful to know a little bit about what is in each one.

Chapter 1: The writer

This chapter introduces the first key concept, text work/identity work, as a means of understanding the requirements of scholarly publication. First-person narratives from early career researchers exemplify the complex tangle of issues involved in writing for publication.

Chapter 2: The reader

This chapter offers a second key concept, that of a specific reader in a discourse community. Our adaption of Fairclough's three layers of discourse is used to explain the difference between a thesis and a journal article. We discuss the importance of choosing the right journal and writing for its readers. A strategy – reading the journal – is explained as a way to become familiar with a particular journal community.

Chapter 3: What's the contribution?

This chapter examines the third key concept, the contribution made by an article as an offering in an ongoing conversation with the discourse community. Through extracts of interviews with editors, we offer a strategy to locate the contribution. A four-part framework for writing abstracts – Tiny Texts – is developed and illustrated to show how the contribution can be made clear to readers.

Chapter 4: So what? Who cares?

Continuing the work on abstracts, this chapter shows how the three key concepts – text work/identity work, a specific discourse community and the contribution – come together in the initial writing of abstracts and their revision. We focus on the writing done by early career academics and offer a strategy for getting started. Before and after texts are used to show the kinds of shifts that can be made through the use of Tiny Texts. We conclude by looking at titles as a crunching strategy to nail the So what of the article.

Chapter 5: Beginning work

This chapter addresses the agony of starting an article and explores how abstracts can also be used as a planning tool, which allows writing to proceed in chunks compatible with academic workloads and work conditions. We offer three strategies for beginning the journal article: Create a Research Space (CARS); Occupy a Research Space (OARS) and Sentence Skeletons, or modelling on expert writers.

Chapter 6: Refining the argument

We begin this chapter by distinguishing between revising, editing and refining. We propose refining as a more productive strategy for doing the middle and end work of an article. We introduce four strategies for refining: mapping the ground, naming the moves, developing a meta-commentary and crunching the conclusion.

Chapter 7: Engaging with reviewers and editors

This chapter considers what writers need to do after their article is returned from the review process. It canvasses the kinds of feedback that writers typically receive from journals. It explains and interrogates the views of publishers, reviewers and the reviewed and introduces the critical role of publication brokers in the revise and resubmit process. Finally, it illustrates strategies for decoding reviewer reports and writing to the editor.

Chapter 8: Writing with others

We now move from thinking about the single article. This chapter opposes the conventional notion of the lone academic writer by exploring different types of writing collaboration. It uses interviews from experienced co-authors to tease out the benefits and complexities. It also considers the problem of asymmetrical collaborations in the research team and in mentor–mentee relationships.

Chapter 9: Living hand to mouse

It is important for academic writers to see themselves as having both a research and a writing agenda which are mutually supportive. Taking a long-term view is crucial, we suggest, for the ongoing text work/identity work of scholarship. We discuss how to mine the thesis for publications and then offer a strategy for continuing publication planning. We also advocate the utility of reviewing, and of working with writing mates and writing groups.

Taken together, these chapters will provide readers with the understandings and strategies necessary for building a scholarly writing profile and career. We encourage its use as a companion to and for their own academic publication, not simply as a report of activities that have 'worked' for others.

Chapter 1

The writer

C. Wright Mills' (1999) axiom of the importance of the imagination to the practices of social science has something helpful to offer to those interested in academic publishing. Mills argued that social sciences requires its practitioners to shift perspectives – from the personal and individualised to the social and historical, from isolated events to those that are connected and contextualised. This move – from one way of seeing things to another – is precisely what needs to happen in the case of academic writing. Writing with the intention of producing knowledge is a process of sense-making. It is not mechanical. One does not simply take a set of findings, or synthesised literatures, and then report. The scholar needs to imagine how the data that they have analysed can be transformed into a persuasive text; they need to imagine themselves not just as an academic colleague in a local setting, but as someone who communicates with unseen and distant peers; they need to see their individual work as part of a broader scholarly endeavour.

We can think about the writing imagination as a kind of everyday creativity. By this, we do not mean the same kind of creativity that is exercised by great novelists, painters and sculptors, but rather the kind of creativity that is exercised by the cook who sees how to turn a bottom shelf of apparently miscellaneous vegetables into a tasty meal, or by the gardener who can visualise the ways in which seeds will grow into a pleasing aesthetic display come summertime. This is creativity which relies both on design and on improvisation, adapting what is available to construct a mental picture of something new, something that is both possible and desirable. This kind of creativity can be defined as 'imaginative activity fashioned so as to produce outcomes that are both original and of value' (National Advisory Committee on Creative and Cultural Education (NACCCE), 1999), with the original and valued outcomes in question here being scholarly writing in the form of journal articles.

In this book we ask readers to take up Mills' axiom and imagine themselves as engaged in a creative practice as published writers. Not just people who publish – not just people who communicate what they've been doing and thinking – but writers who produce a text that speaks cogently to a particular audience of academic peers. As we will explain in this book, the process of composing an academic journal article is to engage in an imaginative shift of perspective – from a set of 'stuff' to an argument that is persuasive and engaging.

The scholarly writer's creative process is specific to the academy. So the imagination required is one which simultaneously envisages the scholar conversing with peers and the text that carries the conversation. This means that the scholar imagines an argument, a way of dialoguing *and* packaging the argument for a particular disciplinary community *and* submitting that work so that it finds its way to print.

Clearly, the kind of imaginative process that is needed to become published changes, depending on both the field and career stage of the writer. For example, a doctoral researcher can generally see themselves writing for examiners and beyond to a journal with a small, friendly readership. Practitioner researchers can easily see themselves writing for peers engaged in similar practices, but generally need to move beyond this to 'see' how the work has broader significance. More experienced scholars have a different horizon of possibility and may know that they should be aiming for a highly ranked journal or one outside their normal field. In each case it takes a leap of imagination to consider the move from where-I-am-now to where-I-might-go and who-I-might-become.

In this chapter we explain why academic writing is inextricably part of the formation of an academic identity. We introduce the first key concept that underpins our approach – text work/identity work.

An academic identity

One of the most over-used concepts in contemporary social science is that of identity (Du Gay *et al.*, 2000). Using the notion of identity here runs the risk of saying nothing and everything at the same time. We therefore do need to note how we understand the term. And now a health warning. What follows is some theoretical writing. If it is too early in the book for this kind of explication, skip to the section on page 18 called 'The necessity of writing'!

Identity is not the same as individuality. Identity is a social and cultural category; it is not a cluster of individual traits such as envy or greed. As a social category, a given identity applies to a group of members. The group is also made in and through whatever the identity category it is known by and for (Hacking, 2006), be it mechanic, mother, or scholar. This is because a particular identity category governs our behaviour in as much as we respond to the expectations and norms that are inherent in the identity category itself. Even if we choose to modify the expectations and conventions attached to an identity category, our actions and intentions shape the ways in which we conceive of ourselves and our work. As Appiah (2005: 66) puts it, identity labels

> operate to mold what we may call identification, the process through which individuals shape their projects – including their plans for their own lives and their conceptions of the good life – by reference to available labels, available identities. In identification, I shape my life by the thought that something is an appropriate aim or an appropriate way of acting.

When we consider the label 'scholar', we think about what it means generally, what the expectations are of scholars and what are the norms of behaviour. We suggest that writing is integral to the identity of 'scholar'. We are expected to write, and to write particular kinds of texts. Being a scholar means taking up the writing project as a means of identifying ourselves with the category itself.

Appiah (2005: 66–71) argues that there are three aspects to the formation of a collective identity:

(1) There must be a readily available term that can be used as an identity 'label'. This identity 'label' means that individuals can be seen by others, inside and outside, as members of the group. The label also makes it possible for a definition to be developed so that there is some consensus about what this identity means – what the group does, what it stands for, what its characteristics are and so on. Members are assumed to do a particular kind of work which is seen as having a particular kind of value. The label 'scholar' allows us/a group of people to be seen by others as engaged in intellectual activities, participating in 'the life of the mind'. In other words, scholar is a social category and in one way and another we are defined by a social conception of scholar-ship.

(2) An identity label is not just something that is applied by one group to another. The identity category is also internalized – a person identifies as a member of the group. So we can think of ourselves as scholars, albeit good or bad or developing. We might of course want to debate what the label scholar means and this is likely to be a debate of significant interest to all those within the community that identify as scholars. But this kind of debate may be seen as 'irrelevant' or simply 'navel gazing' by those outside.

(3) A social identity is always accorded a particular pattern of external social behaviour. Car salesmen are treated with suspicion, doctors with some deference. Scholars may be seen as living in an 'ivory tower', with the assumption that we always have our heads stuck in a book.

We also understand that people are given, and take up an identity category through imbuing it with their own meaning-making narrative. The narrative might go something like: This is the story of how I got to be a real estate salesman/doctor/scholar. This is what I do every day as a real estate salesman/doctor/scholar. As a real estate salesman/doctor/scholar I behave in a particular way and believe in particular things because that's what we real estate salesmen/doctors/scholars do.

Let us take this a little further. We can say that the work of identification, the ongoing construction of an identity, is accomplished via a narrative of the self (Bruner, 1986; MacIntyre, 1984; C. Taylor, 1989). An *identity narrative* functions as a meaning-making device which brings isolated events, experiences, relationships, memories and perspectives together into a story that seems to have coherence, logic and unity. An identity narrative is always constructed in reference to wider social narratives, but also to the social category and to other people – from direct feedback and from our best guesses about how we think others see us. It is the product of unconscious and conscious processes of reflection. An identity narrative is both a public and private representation – it is how we explain our category-selves to our-self as well as to others. This category representation may well change depending on who we are talking to and in what circumstances. Identity is also a productive story – it produces and reproduces the self in the telling. Because of this malleable quality, any identity is never fixed but always in formation. And because of this provisionality, identity stories are always more or less open to change.

Contemporary theorists working in a range of traditions hold that the notion of a singular and unified identity is misleading (e.g. Bauman, 2004; Braidotti, 2011; Game and Metcalfe, 1996). The narrative of a 'self' is literally a fabrication. All of us have multiple identities which overlap, intermingle, and some can even remain relatively separate from each other. Parent, child, worker, student, friend, professional, member of various communities – each of these categorical associations brings with it its own expectations and its own identification narrative, its own persona, its own representation of what it means to be this kind of person, doing this kind of activity, in this place and at this time.

The narrativised self is not a neutral account. It is itself a cultural construction, shaped and framed by prevailing norms, conventions and mores. But it also emanates from a constellation of morals and ethics that acts as a foundation for action. Our values and beliefs govern what we think it means to be a person living in a particular society with particular obligations, rights and responsibilities. Furthermore, the self embodies a way of knowing about and living in the world. This knowing is social, and draws on the kinds of communities of which we are part, and with which we identify and claim membership. To take up a feminist identity, for example, means to always see the world – and 'be' (live, work, play) in a world – that is gendered. To be an Australian means that it is impossible to avoid the understanding that everyday life is indelibly stained by colonialism and its consequences. In short, and taking a philosophical stance, we suggest that an identity is not only ontological, but also epistemological and axiological.

Following this, we can then say that a *scholarly* identity is a narrative which brings to the category of scholar an individual biography of events, relationships, experiences, memories and perspectives derived from life in and around higher education. It is the way we scholars make sense of our lives and our work in the academy to others and to ourselves. The scholarly identification narrative creates an apparently seamless account of a career trajectory through a social world of knowledge production, debates and collegialities, feuds and affiliations and institutional contexts.

The scholarly identity is rooted in our perceptions of how others view scholars in general. Being an academic is not necessarily always a good thing. Intellectual work may on the one hand have high status, but on the other its practitioners can also be seen as elitist and isolationist/isolated. Indeed, the term academic is often used as a pejorative equating to someone who is removed from reality, self-indulgent, obfuscatory, obtuse and perhaps even redundant (Dunant, 1994). The same kinds of pejorative terms are used about academic writing, a point we take up in Chapter 2. It's probably just as well that we don't rely entirely on these more general views of academics and that the scholarly identity is also comprised of our perceptions of how others like us see us and our particular teaching and scholarship. As we get direct feedback from supervisors, colleagues and students, as well as from conscious/unconscious processes of reflection, we weld together these bits and pieces of information to produce an identity narrative about ourself as scholar.

A scholarly identity is both a public and private representation. It is what we tell ourselves in private as well as what we say to others. It is productive and reproductive of what we do and what we will become. And thus, our scholarly selves, like other identities or aspects of our identity, are always in formation, always about histories and presents but also about becomings and potentialities, more or less open to change.

Scholarly identities are often formed in relation to ascribed stages: doctoral, postdoctoral, early career, mid-career, mature and senior. These sub-categories make assumptions about a linear progression and growth. Actual years and levels of readiness are often attributed to each stage; the arbitrariness of this becomes clear when we see that different countries and institutions ascribe different times to different stages. For example, five years after the doctorate no longer qualifies as early career in Australia whereas in the UK early career lasts for six years. There is also an implied progression in these stages: the scholar moves from one to the other improving as she goes, starting out as a relatively empty apprentice scholarly vessel and ending up replete with wisdom. This progressively enlightened and Enlightenment view of scholarship is a superficial and misleading developmental discourse. It assumes commonalities of experience which simply do not stack up in the modern university where a variety of entry points and career pathways exist (McAlpine and Akerlind, 2010). It also assumes that people sit neatly in one category, whereas in reality they may well straddle more than one 'stage'. While ostensibly being in one stage, it is possible for a scholar to actually be/feel/do something from another 'stage' earlier or later. While we use 'stage' language in this text, we are very aware that these are loaded and somewhat unsatisfactory terms.

Like other identities, the 'scholar' is also strongly values-based and institutionally framed. Current debates about the role of the scholar, the purposes of knowledge production and the functions of a university are now commonplace across the world (e.g. Baert and Shipman, 2005; Delanty, 2001; Holmwood, 2011; Readings, 1996). What counts as a 'good' – or not so good – scholar is contentious. We sit with those who see a social purpose for higher education and are concerned with this being reduced to a narrow, instrumentalist view of economic benefits and short-term impact. We are also concerned about how this view of scholars and scholarly work plays out in and as writing.

The necessity of writing

There is no escaping the fact that the identity of scholar and the practice of scholarship are tangled in writing. The title 'professor' which is, in many countries, a general salutation given to all of those who teach in a university regardless of their seniority, literally means one who professes. A professor is someone who not only has an allegiance to a particular mode of thought/ creed/way of life, but also explains, advocates and stands by it. In the context of higher education, what is professed is a field of knowledge production; this may be, for example, a discipline or a particular interpretation of a field, or a combined epistemological/ontological/axiological position.

Professors, taken inclusively, profess in a range of ways, but primarily through their teaching and their research. Writing is a key practice in professing. It is one major way through which professors make their concerns and commitments and expertise known to the wider world, and in the first instance, to colleagues in the scholarly community. It is impossible to consider that, in contemporary times, professing might be something that could be done without publication, because this is the major and accepted means through which knowledge is transferred from the private sphere of analysis into public conversation, scrutiny and recognition.

This is an important perspective to remember in times when publication has an apparent market value. Universities in many countries are now assessed and funded on their productivity, measured by the quantum of collective publications that their professors produce, their citation rates and positions in various kinds of league tables. This has made publication a high-stakes activity, and all of us are under pressure to produce publications of 'quality', however that is measured. Our institutions these days depend on our professing labour for income, reputation and enrolments.

In this context, the journal article seems to operate as a kind of quasi-'gold standard' of publication, since it does go through a process of peer review which is held to be a kind of community seal of approval. If the article is 'good' it meets the criteria for writing and research as judged by two or more colleagues in the field. The performative and marketised focus on publication often seems to obliterate the singular importance of publication as a means of collective knowledge production. It transforms the historical gift economy of the academy into something much more instrumental.

Yet, at the same time, it is important to acknowledge the ways in which professors and their writing are seen outside of the forensic regimes of measurement and reward. While publications count significantly for promotions in higher education, we want to focus here on the ways in which professing still occurs via writing and publication. As scholars we are known for and by our research and publications. We can say that the text is one representation of the scholar – who we are as well as what we know. Readers form views about scholars and their scholarship through texts. They make evaluations about the work and the scholar at the same time. Sometimes readers are engaged in dialogue with writers who are dead, but who live on through their publications. Most often of course, the writer is simply someone who is contemporary but who lives somewhere else, with whom readers nevertheless engage in conversation through reading and then through take up and use of their ideas.

Writing is, we suggest, a key way for us to make ourselves as scholars and to create a scholarly identity (see also Casanave and Vandrick, 2003; Ivanic, 1998). As we craft a text and shape an argument, we are also crafting and shaping our scholarly self. As we write, we are enacting a particular imagined view of our selves – who we are and who we want to be. Through our writings we present ourselves and thus are known for particular things – not just for an area of work, but also perhaps for 'getting off the fence' (Griffiths, 1998), or staying firmly on it; for having interesting ideas and perspectives – or not; for making important or inconsequential contributions. Through writing, professors literally make their mark on their chosen field. This is a far cry from seeing writing as something required, or something which requires simply going through the motions of making a contribution.

It is the Gordian knot of scholarship and scholarly identity which makes writing so challenging. But while possibly frightening, it is actually the combination of text work/identity work which also allows us to produce ourselves, to evolve or stagnate, to take a stand or to duck for cover, to imagine ourselves as speaking about something we hold to be important and significant to a few people who live locally, or conversing with an international community who may or may not have heard of us before. This capacity to imagine oneself as an authoritative scholar engaged in an ongoing conversation with others, and the text as the means of connecting with others and saying something that matters, is central to the publication process.

The implications of the 'join' between text and identity, with its affective and ontological dimensions, are key to the approach we take in this book. The notion of text work/identity work is what marks our approach off from those who see publication as a technical process of writing development.

Textualising the scholarly self

There is a deep connection between the scholarly identity and the text. We write an article in our disciplines; we locate the work in recent literatures, we analyse data, we use the data to substantiate our argument. But we are never just writing the article. We are also simultaneously writing our self. We project a scholar onto the page and convey a relationship with our material and with the broader readership we are addressing. We may be confident or tentative; clear or overly embedded, fuzzy or hiding because we are nervous that others may disagree with or challenge our work.

The writing identity link is not often talked about in universities because it is difficult to see. The text, on the other hand, is tangible. The journal article has a materiality – of word length, margin width, page design. It appears in a journal with a cover, an index, a title and an abstract. The writer's name appears in print accompanied by a brief bio. This is the text. But the process of writing that text, of drafting and crafting and struggling to find the right words has material effects. It creates the scholar who, at the end of writing, will be different to the writer who began. Perhaps a bit more knowing and confident, perhaps still worried about having something worthy to say, perhaps a bit bolder and willing to take greater risks.

When we think about the scholarly identity being formed in and through writing, it is not hard to understand why early career writers might find writing for journals difficult. Writing a text *and* writing a self is hard labour. Writers often struggle because they are negotiating text work and identity work at the *same* time. But they often opt for a more self-deprecating explanation, namely that they are just not good enough or smart enough. They feel ashamed that writing is hard and imagine everyone else does it easily. They are reluctant to speak about such matters publically, lest they be pigeonholed as a struggler.

This was apparent when Barbara attended a small working conference in 2006 to present an early version of our text work/identity work framework to a group of professors from Australia, the UK and the US. The aim was to present chapters-in-progress for a joint international publication and receive feedback for subsequent revising. Ten doctoral students also attended from the local host institution to participate in the discussions (see Kamler and Thomson, 2007, for the chapter that eventuated from this meeting).

Barbara remembers well the silence that greeted her presentation. Very interesting, the professors said, this idea that doctoral students might be engaged in both text work and identity work and that this could explain some of their difficulties with writing. But they had few questions and seemed uninterested in the implications for doctoral supervision. Barbara was upset by this lack of engagement. But then at morning break as she ventured into the ladies' room, she was barraged by six excited doctoral students who wanted to discuss the identity work/text work nexus. They felt unable to speak in public – and rarely admitted their worries to their supervisors. A lively discussion followed in this private space away from the professors.

We have often reflected on the absurdity of this conversation occurring in the ladies' toilet. Why was our notion of the identity struggles that accompany text formation private women's business? And why were these junior academics too afraid to discuss these matters in front of their senior colleagues? We believe this is a striking example – and not just a metaphor – of the privatisation of discussions about writing in universities. While academics may complain privately about the obstacles they face in writing books, articles, or grants, there is a studied institutional silence about such things and a dearth of approaches for discussing the actual complexities and tasks involved.

For us the text work/identity work framework provides a productive way to open up discussion and theorising about what is at stake for writers (outside of shame and failure discourses), particularly for those who are novice in their disciplines.

Text work/identity work: two examples

When we decided to write this book, we asked some researchers with whom we have worked to write narratives about themselves as writers. We asked them to think about *where* they were up to as well as *what* they were up to in their writing and publication. Here we introduce two of those people, Kerry and Simon.

Kerry

Kerry is now working as a lecturer in education having finished a PhD as a mature student. At the time of writing for us she was two years away from her PhD and had published several articles before and during her candidature. She has just published the book of her PhD entitled *Schoolgirl pregnancy, motherhood and education: Dealing with difference* (Vincent, 2012). Her reflection shows the trajectory of her identity formation and its dependence on doing and getting support for the text work.

My identity as a writer feels like it is still in its early stages. It is my identity as a teacher, a psychologist and a researcher that have overshadowed this other emerging identity, even though each of these roles has required me to write. It also feels like it has also been a very long and slow process.

I know I left secondary school not being able to write and I recall failing my first written assignment at university. I was not from a family of scholars or university goers but I thought I could do better – if only I knew how. I went to my tutor. No doubt he will have long forgotten this but I still feel grateful for the time that a then very young Hugh Lauder took to patiently talk me through some basics; an essay has an introduction, a middle and a conclusion. I began paying more attention to structure in what I read and what I wrote. This experience also taught me that writing skills can be developed. Both of those things contributed to my future identity as a writer.

When, many years later, I completed my Masters dissertation, my supervisor suggested I publish something from it. I needed no further encouragement, but that was not because I saw myself as a writer, it was because I had something I felt passionate about that I thought needed to be said. I wrote for my first audience. An article was duly published but I considered this to be a one-off. I was a psychologist in training, not a writer. But people emailed me and I learned that getting something published can be quite a good way of getting people to think about something. I had moved a little further along the path to a writer identity.

Years later still, I had a short period working as a research fellow. Positive comments from others about my contributions to co-authored work made me think, 'Oh, maybe I'm OK at this'. But writers are professors, or at the very least have Dr in front of their name – or they are people who write for a living. I enjoyed research but I was not so sure about writing. Nevertheless, during this time the PhD seed had been sown and some years later, motivated primarily by my desire to stay working in HE, I did embark upon a PhD. I understood that both the PhD process, and working in HE, necessarily involved both research and writing.

Two important things emerge from Kerry's identification narrative. First, she sees that scholarly writing is integral to being a member of the social category of scholar. As a self-confessed 'non-writer' who wrote, she did not see herself as belonging to this group. Her narrative is one where, in retrospect, she is able to see how she began the process of becoming a scholarly writer because she understood that this was the price of admission. Second, this is a narrative of learning, of getting better and more familiar with the writing tasks required of scholarship. As she identified more with the category of scholar, she could see how each writing task brought her more 'inside' the group. She adopted and internalised the norms of the category.

Getting something from my PhD published was another important milestone. There seemed little point researching something unless the findings were made accessible to a wider audience – but what helped make this actually happen was encouragement and support from my supervisor to first present at a conference, and then subsequently to develop this work into a journal article.

The conference experience taught me that some people were actually interested in what I had to say. The next bit, getting something published, was about writing. It was about saying it in a way that was judged as good enough by those who were already part of the academic community. As someone part way through a PhD, I was aspiring to become part of that community. Presenting at a conference and getting through the peer-review process were both important for building confidence as a writer and in helping me to feel part of this wider community. Possibly key for someone such as myself who lacked confidence in my own writing, these moves were underpinned by supervisory support – including being told by a prolific writer whose work I enjoyed and respected, that I can write. Hearing or reading about the challenges, pain and uncertainties of other writers was also important. I came to see that I was not alone in these experiences – they are part of the process.

More recently, delivering a seminar on some of my work to ex-colleagues provided an important reminder that other people might well be interested in what I have to say. That motivates me to write. It makes me think that it is worth the time and the effort getting those findings and ideas into the public domain. And as I complete a book based around my PhD research, I recognise that sole authorship will be another important milestone as will, at some later point, getting something else published without feeling that I have leaned unduly on my writing mentor. Both of these are about growing confidence and a need to 'stand on one's own two feet' as a writer. It is in these ways that I anticipate moving further along this path.

Kerry has written a biographical sketch of her formation as a writer. She points to growth, change, people who were important, and what they did to facilitate her growth. She captures key moments and processes, demonstrating a strong meta-view of her own learning. This is a positive narrative. It is not one which focuses on the struggles to write; it is one which accepts that membership of the identity category of scholar brings with it the requirement to write and to continue to develop that writing. This is an enabling narrative, which positions Kerry as continuing to act in accordance with the internal and external norms and conventions of the identity of scholar. Of course there were struggles and negative experiences, and plenty of them. But in moving to explain her identity trajectory through this biographical sketch, a good way for any scholar to reflect on the tangles of text work/identity work, she gains distance, which enables her to focus on the progress made, rather than on the stumbles and anxieties.

Simon

Simon could be called an early career researcher. At the time of writing for us he was three years away from the PhD hurdle, and had worked for all of that time as a contract researcher. While his PhD was in education, all of his paid work was in health sociology and so his publications consisted at the time of three refereed articles from his doctorate, the first of which was co-authored with his supervisor. His other publications were from his paid work where he was inevitably second or third in a list of authors, behind the permanent academics leading the projects. Here Simon reflects on what it means to publish and how the press for publication is in tension with his imaginary of the kind of scholar self he wants to become.

> Even though I have produced a body of work, I don't describe myself as a writer, partly through my lack of what might be called 'market output', but also through my lack of contribution to a public voice. I've had quite a long romance with the idea of being a writer, and for a long time I've written through various forms; diaries, letters, poems, songs. Yet I would never consider publishing any of these, they are private pleasures. I flirted with journalism before studying sociology, but hated the conventions and didn't much like the idea of being a jobbing reporter. Then sociology provided me with a new will to write as well as the possible means to finding a market for that writing.
>
> However, many of the conventions I encountered in writing my PhD seemed to have a rationale that was not immediately underlined by the need for a market, but more by the need to take seriously and responsibly

one's own representations. Attempting to enter the world of academic publishing, however, seems to push these considerations back to the margins, giving way once again to economic considerations. I think in terms of the writing work of publishing, these conventions take time and experience to gain facility with. They are dull and inflexible. Yet they can be acquired at fairly little 'expense' – and so in some sense I do feel like I'm on the way to getting the publishing thing 'sorted'. However, they also require a certain advanced 'knowing'; a vision which sees both an argument and a place for that argument. Through the PhD I had grown much more accustomed to exploratory writing and emergent arguments.

In my case I think this is where the writing work of publishing collides with the identity work; as the exploratory and emergent are both key building blocks for me, as academic identities and as ways of seeing and being in the world. I see the creative work of academia (reading, researching, writing) as a means of exploring possibility, and I see one's responsibility in being in the world as recognising possibility. This may be to say that I self-identify as a writer even though I do not use it to signify my-self to others.

Under contract research conditions I do find the writing work a struggle; the physical availability of time and space, the journal conventions, the frequent lack of fit between contract work and academic aspirations, and the unsupportive manager, are all battles in themselves. But I think my struggles with actually putting words out into the market are as much about these itches of identification; insecurities about value, merit and responsibility, insecurities which I did gain some comfort with through the writing of the PhD, but which often require suppression in order to put work out to be published. Currently, I think I can perform this suppression on the basis that if I put enough product out I may attain a position of greater freedom in the future. Textual outputs of all kinds should be more than the satisfaction of personal ambition or romantic ideals, they should be public goods; which means more than making them publically available.

Simon addresses the norms of the social category of scholar and how various institutional and ethical expectations sit together. He talks about the purposes of scholarship – 'a contribution to a public good' and of writings as 'public goods' – and the importance of professing – 'a will to write', 'the responsibility of being in the world'. He uses a model of scholarship as a becoming and himself as a scholar in formation – 'exploratory writings and emergent arguments' – and these as 'key building blocks' of his scholarly identity. He suggests that his writings emanate from an imaginary, 'a vision which sees both an argument and a place for that argument'. However, he notes that, because of the performative pressures around publishing, it is not always possible to write what and how he imagines himself to be. These desires become a set of 'itches' that he perhaps cannot always scratch.

Our reading of the passage suggests that Simon's writing (re)presents scholarship, the obligation to profess, and writing and publishing as inter-dependent, mutually constructed and reinforcing. This is text work/identity work as a lived reality of membership of the collective group 'scholar'.

We now move from researchers reflecting on their 'progress' as writers, to consider how text work/identity work appears in and as writing.

Identity struggles over and in the text

The following journal article abstract was written by Gerri, an early career researcher in social work who had recently completed a project on elder abuse. Her abstract illustrates a key point we are making: that identity issues surface in the text and are visible to readers as 'troubled text'.

Risky business: the experiences of community-based aged care professionals working in cases of suspected elder abuse

While the issue of elder abuse has gained prominence in Australia in recent years, little is known about the experiences and views of practi-tioners working in this area, a perspective essential for the development of elder abuse policy and guidelines. This paper addresses that gap and reports on a study exploring the experiences of sixteen aged care pro-fessionals working in situations of suspected elder abuse across a range of community-based agencies. Three main themes are identified in workers' accounts. The first concerns the competing practice frameworks employed by workers, with risk management dominating, followed by therapeutic and family violence approaches. The second theme centres on the practice challenges experienced by workers including judging capacity, client self-determination and inter-agency collaboration. The final theme highlights the professional and personal costs of this work to the workers themselves. The paper concludes with recommendations for elder abuse policy and guidelines, including the need for specific elder abuse policies, an identified lead agency to coordinate a multi-agency approach, and a clearly articulated framework for elder abuse practice.

Abstract 1.1 Gerri struggles to take a stand

It is clear to us that identity issues are being struggled over in this abstract, but we don't know exactly what they are. They are not transparent to the reader. What we do know is that something is 'not quite right'. This does not mean that the abstract is badly written. On the contrary, the writing is fluent and clearly stated. The sentences are sequentially ordered and the syntax signals a defined structure. Gerri begins by identifying a gap – an absence of work on elder abuse from the point of view of social work practitioners. She then constructs what appears to be a scientific report in detached third-person language. She identifies three themes based on her systematic analytic work, and on the basis of these makes a claim for new policy guidelines and a framework for elder abuse practice. Thus we find all the mechanics of scholarship in the abstract, but we can ask: where is the writer? What does she think? Gerri appears to be hiding behind the text. In our analysis:

- the claims made don't connect with the focus of the article
- there doesn't appear to be a way to get from the three themes to the claims at the end
- the claims appear bigger than the evidence would warrant
- the researcher's viewpoint is entirely missing – there is nothing distinctive being offered.

This appears to be a problem of writer identity: it's about who the writer is in her profession; about getting the courage to name an issue and stand out in the field so that she is visible and making a case. What she offers is a three-part genre: *I did the study, I found three themes, I conclude that.* To the extent that the abstract articulates a point of view, Gerri attributes opinion to the practitioners who have been interviewed. We call this ventriloquising. The interviewees have something to say, not the writer of the article. She hopes that they will say everything that is needed.

It would be possible to approach this text as a writing development issue and suggest the writer put in the link between the claim and the conclusion – that is, she improve the surface of the text. This is not the tack that Barbara took. She met with Gerri to discuss the abstract and asked questions to evoke what appeared to be her missing point of view. Conversation ranged widely for ten or fifteen minutes until the issue of family violence emerged. Gerri explained that the dominant way of viewing the harm done to elders was from a framework of victim abuse, where the solution was to make things better for the victim. A view of elder abuse as family violence, by contrast, shifted the blame to the system in which the abuse occurs – to the family rather than the victim. Gerri became quite energised as she discussed the implications of naming the family as perpetrator of the violence. Her interviewees also found this naming shift significant, as there would be multiple consequences for social work action and policy – for reporting violence – and for punishing those who perpetrate it. As Gerri articulated a point of view that was missing in her writing, Barbara asked how she felt about making this argument in the article itself. There was a long pause, then she said: 'I'd love to but I'm terrified. It would upset the previous ways of handling elder abuse . . . but I'd love to'.

We see this conversation as creating a space for Gerri to take up Mills' axiom and engage in an imaginative shift of perspective. As her viewpoint surfaced and she was assisted to name the issue, her fear and excitement were palpable. It was thrilling for Gerri to imagine herself as a scholar taking a stand so that things might change, but terrifying to move against convention and be seen as a critic of current policy. We understand this struggle as quintessential identity work. The unsatisfactory abstract is the identity struggle made material – a report of what happened with no argument. Gerri is as yet unable to imagine herself naming the real issue or imagine herself as the kind of scholar who can speak bravely to her field.

In subsequent drafts of the abstract and article this is exactly what she decided to strive for.

So what, now what?

We have suggested that scholarly writing is not a simple process, nor is it a question of finding a 'fix' for a set of technical problems. For this reason, there is little point in pathologising people who have difficulties with writing – creating syndromes, and on that basis, solutions – when the issue is one of text work/identity work. However, there is no quick or simple answer to the identity–text problems that are manifest in and through writing. Rather, we suggest, the approach must be one which begins with recognising the tangle of values, imaginaries, obligations and expectations of self and others that characterise scholarship at all levels. The task is to help the writer imagine themselves as an authoritative scholar and write/speak accordingly. In the next chapter we discuss the first steps in becoming less tentative. It might seem counterintuitive, but we say it's through a focus on *who* we want to read what we are writing, rather than on the writing itself.

Chapter 2

The reader

If you were to come into one of our workshops you would hear us asking participants over and over, 'Who is the reader? Who is the reader? Who is the reader?'

We are surprised that this question startles so many people. Often people just don't know. They haven't thought of this as important. Sometimes people have a journal in mind but can actually say nothing in answer to who reads it. Other times we are told something like – the readers are other social workers, teacher educators, paramedics, university administrators. While this is a start towards answering our question, it is actually inadequate to the task. Our contention is that it is impossible to write a journal article without knowing where it is going and the precise nature of the readership.

In this chapter we explain why by outlining the second key concept in this book, that of the discourse community. We show how this concept provides not only a framework, but also a strategy for beginning to write a journal article.

We begin, however, by clarifying the underlying theory which sits behind the notion of a discourse community.

Writing as a social, discursive practice

In Chapter 1 we talked about writing as an act of imagination and creativity. It is important here not to lapse into a notion of creativity and imagination as coming from a unique individual who exists somehow outside of their social context. As an imaginative act, writing is similarly not an individual practice, something that is done in the confinement of the lonely garret. Writing is always socially situated.

By this we mean that writers are always writing for someone. What they write is shaped by a set of rules, expectations and conventions. What it is possible to say, and how it is said, are shaped and framed – governed perhaps – by often implicit, taken-for-granted understandings.

Rules and conventions are not necessarily arbitrary and unpleasant. Academic rules and conventions have evolved over time in particular communities where there are specific ways of thinking, speaking, being, talking and writing. Such communities might, for example, be disciplinary. The ways in which a psychologist frames a problem, what is included and excluded, named and framed, are based in over one hundred years of scholarly activity which have built up a set of traditions. We might think of these as ways of thinking, writing and doing psychology – and as we argued in the last chapter, of being a psychologist.

This thinking, writing, doing and being activity will differ considerably from discipline to discipline (Deane and O'Neill, 2011). Thinking, writing, doing and being in the discipline of sociology differs from that in philosophy or economics. There are also sub-groupings which operate similarly across and within disciplines. Linguistics, for example, has evolved a number of specific sub-groupings – corpus linguistics, transformational grammar, systemic functional linguistics and so on – each of which has a core set of understandings, problematisations, terminologies and analytic tools and approaches.

Internal disciplinary rules and conventions serve to bind members together and also to mark off those who do not belong. What can be seen by outsiders as 'academic jargon' is actually a specialised 'insider' language which has specific meanings to those who exist within the community. This is not to negate the importance of speaking and writing differently when communicating with people 'outside' of the community. But we can think of these shared 'internal' understandings and languages as allowing the community to do its work (Culler and Lamb, 2003), rather than a failure to speak plainly or some addiction to speaking in tongues.

Part of the work of doctoral study involves being inducted into disciplinary communities to learn the accepted ways of thinking, speaking and writing. It is not uncommon for the first response to be a feeling of inadequacy or a rejection of texts and traditions. The first time, for example, that doctoral researchers encounter social theory can be overwhelming; what do all of these peculiar terms actually mean? But as more literatures are read and absorbed, these terms become familiar, as do their common usages. When doctoral researchers say particular specialised words out loud for the first time, the effects can be positively visceral – they feel annoyed, vulnerable, awkward and sometimes fake. If they persist, then they become part of their specific scholarly community and this is marked by the facility with which they speak and write as 'insiders'. They become, as Bourdieu (1990) puts it, 'fish in water', and as the discipline's ways of thinking, writing, doing and being become more and more 'natural', these specialised terms tend to disappear from view.

Early career researchers have generally cottoned on to the broad dimensions of discourse communities and they can talk the talk, but they do not necessarily know how these play out around particular journals and the task of writing the journal article.

The issue is that writing for journals is writing into and for a very specific discourse community. What is less obvious, perhaps, is that the community has ways of ensuring relative conformity amongst members. In journals, the most obvious ways in which this happens is through a process of refereeing. We address the refereeing process throughout the remainder of this book.

We now offer a way of thinking about how the writer needs to engage with specific journal discourse communities.

Three layers: a metaphor for understanding journal writing

We find the work of Norman Fairclough (1989, 1995, 2003) useful in visualising how discourse communities, writers and texts interact. Here we reprise our earlier interpretation of Fairclough's model of social discursive practice as it applies to the doctoral thesis (see Kamler and Thomson, 2006, for an earlier version of the three layers). We contrast writing for the doctorate with writing for a journal, explaining as we do so why it is that inexperienced writers struggle to gain acceptance by journal communities.

Fairclough (1992) proposed a three-part interactive structure for understanding language use in its social and cultural context: text, discourse practice and social practice. These layers are interdependent and suggest that no text is ever produced in isolation from its context.

In our interpretation, we see the centre layer as the text, the actual spoken or written span of language that writers or speakers produce. In the outer layer is the broader cultural context, including the discourse community and its specific practices, histories, conventions and expectations. In the middle layer (between the text and the discourse community) sits the mediating practices, where insiders judge and evaluate the text as well as shape and facilitate the text's production.

Figure 2.1 shows how this heuristic applies to the production of a doctoral dissertation. In the centre sits the doctoral thesis, the big book. In the outer layer we find disciplinary conventions, university policies, higher education policies, geographic and national traditions as well as global frameworks, such as the Bologna Agreement. The student who writes the thesis needs to understand this broad context, but is supported in this work by their supervisors or doctoral committee which we find in the middle layer. Supervisors shape the thesis through their comments, conversation, recommendations,

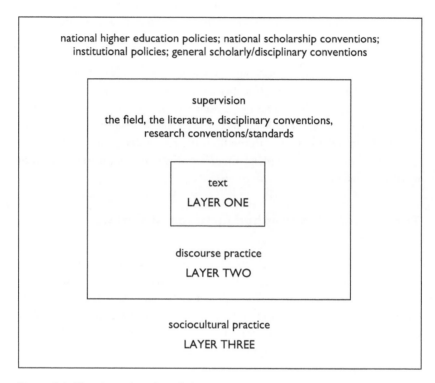

Figure 2.1 The three layers and the thesis

and track-changes on the text. In doing so, they literally embody the broad scholarly and specific disciplinary discourse community and its practices and norms. Increasingly, the student will also be supported and regulated by teachers of various graduate and postgraduate training courses, seminars and workshops. Most importantly, the examiners also sit in this layer and their job is clearly regulatory. They decide which texts are acceptable – or not. They are selected because of their relative standing in the discourse community and therefore their capacity to make decisions on its behalf.

Howard Becker (1986), a renowned sociologist who writes about writing in the social sciences, provides an elegant exemplar of the ways in which doctoral writers need to think about both layer 2 and layer 3 when they are constructing their dissertation text.

One way to understand the problem of writing is to see it in context. We write what we write – in the case at hand, a dissertation – in the context of academic institutions. The problem's solution, in this context, requires not only putting together ideas and evidence clearly and convincingly. It also requires that we satisfy the requirements those institutions insist on for such a document.

The author, the dissertation writer, has first to satisfy the immediate readers, the people who will say yes or no, pass or don't pass, go back and do it again and we'll have another look or, for the lucky ones, 'Well done! Get it published and get on with your life and work.' People who serve as this kind of reader – for the most part reasonable, sane people – still have to consider more than the quality of the work before them. They think about the politics of their departments ('Old George will have an apoplectic fit if you attack his favorite theory') or, more commonly, of the discipline ('I agree with what you have written, but if you take that unpopular position or write in that unconventional style you will have trouble getting your work published') and as a result suggest changes in substance and style that have no reason in logic or taste, but which result purely from academic convention.

(Becker, undated)

Becker clearly identifies layer 2 considerations – the examiners who will pass judgment on the text. He makes visible the need to also consider layer 3, how others in the discourse community will regard the work in relation to their own and to the field. Sometimes people dismiss layer 2 as a hoop to jump through, and layer 3 as simply a set of unnecessary and tiresome politics. While this may be in part correct, it is also the case that these layers are helpful as well as obstructive, enabling as well as regulatory, and that some of these constraints are productive. What is happening is the shaping of the text and the shaping of the scholar within a particular frame. As Becker notes, it is possible to shuck off these conventions and restraints – but only if one is prepared for the consequences. In the case of a doctoral thesis this can be failure from the examiners (layer 2), and mistrust of the scholarship and the scholar (layer 3).

The layers work differently in the case of journal publication.

Figure 2.2 shows how this heuristic applies to producing a journal article. In the centre is the text – the journal article. In the outer layer are the discourse community and a publishing market (if it is a commercial journal). Here, we also find performative regimes enacted through higher education funding policies, citation indices, promotion regulations and audit regimes. The writer of the journal article must amass this layer 3 knowledge in order to select appropriate journals and develop strategic approaches to publishing.

The middle layer in journal publication is densely populated with editors, editorial boards, publishers' representatives, readers and a large community of journal referees. Editors and editorial boards are selected for their standing in

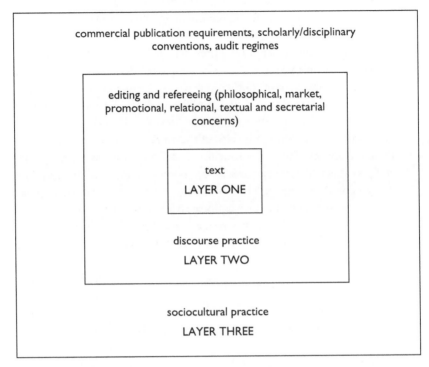

commercial publication requirements, scholarly/disciplinary conventions, audit regimes

editing and refereeing (philosophical, market, promotional, relational, textual and secretarial concerns)

text

LAYER ONE

discourse practice

LAYER TWO

sociocultural practice

LAYER THREE

Figure 2.2 The three layers and the journal article

the discourse community. It is a marker of distinction to be an editor and a sign of peer esteem to be a board member. The community of reviewers, however, is more mixed and may consist of experienced and relatively novice members of the discourse community, as well as people with varying degrees of insider/outsider status. In contrast to the mediation effected through doctoral supervision in the middle layer, there is less support offered to the journal writer in engaging with layer 2.

The vast majority of layer 2 interactions are not face-to-face but conducted by computerised and anonymised submission processes, written feedback and email communication. This is a much less predictable, less supported, less personable, more distanced and more ritualised experience than the doctoral thesis, where the supervision and training process is overtly pedagogical. In journal layer 2, the writer usually feels they have less agency in these transactions and that the results are somewhat unpredictable. Indeed, the term 'lottery' is often used in connection with the refereeing process. Even if this is the case, and there is evidence that it is not (see http://scholarlykitchen.sspnet.org/2011/12/08/is-peer-review-a-coin-toss/), the fact remains that the journal writer must imagine the layer 2 readership in all its specificity and diversity. They must write for *this* journal, *this* editor, *this* editorial board. The writer's agency must be focused on making the text 'fit' with what layer 2 expects and will judge as being of suitable 'quality' for publication (see Chapter 7 for further discussion).

The failure to deal with layer 2 and 3 has serious consequences in relation to journal publication as can be seen in the following case narrative.

Stephen was a medical sociologist who had recently completed his PhD. His doctoral work critiqued a well-known and deeply held practice in general practice medicine. His examiners were medical sociologists and found his approach and his argument convincing and exciting. They urged him to publish. Stephen's first article was written for a highly ranked medical journal and elaborated the key critique he had made in his doctoral research. When the three reviews came he was shocked at the diversity of opinion and the strength of the opposition to his arguments. Some of it was positively vitriolic. His writing clearly challenged layer 3 taken-for-granted wisdom in the field, and some of the reviewers were indignant at his audacity. The journal editor, however, clearly impressed with the quality of Stephen's scholarship, sought further reviews. Stephen revised the article but once again there was further mixed opinion and vitriol. Stephen had a conversation with the editor which canvassed the possibility of a special issue or a forum in which there would be debate, with discussion of Stephen's article by prominent scholars in the medical field. Stephen was happy with this suggestion and had begun a third set of revisions for the special issue when he received a letter from the editor saying that the editorial board had not backed the notion of a special issue. With regret, his article was rejected.

Stephen brought this story to a writing workshop and was genuinely perplexed about why he had been rejected, given the intense interest his work appeared to have generated. Layer 3 we said. Layer 3.

Stephen's story is a clear example of the power of layer 3 – in this case the medical profession – mediated through layer 2, the editorial board and referees – to reject a critique emanating from outside its specific discourse community. Who was a medical sociologist to critique the medical profession? The relative status of the disciplines had everything to do with Stephen's rejection: medicine versus sociology.

In hindsight and through the workshop discussion, Stephen came to see that his decision to submit to this journal was bold but naïve. He had not under-stood the discourses, the threat that his work posed and the resistance from the discipline to outsiders, particularly a cross-disciplinary upstart who had just passed his PhD. Stephen was an interloper in this discourse community and it was the combined efforts of layer 2 and 3 that pushed him away. It was not the quality of his scholarship that was in question. The editor recognised that the work was well conducted and significant. This, however, was insufficient to ensure publication.

The lesson here is clear. The choice of journal is important, but choosing a journal is in reality choosing a reader, a reader who is a member of a specific discourse community.

The importance of deliberate choice

We started this chapter by noting that our first question in workshops is, 'Who is the reader?' We have explained that this question actually means, 'What is the discourse community into which this article is to go, and what might be expected in layers 2 and 3?' Stephen didn't know he had to do this and no one had ever told him. Books on academic publishing generally say choose a journal, but they usually don't examine why this is important, the complexity of making a choice, the process of choosing, or how it is that insider knowledge about particular journals might be acquired. Choice is often seen as a technical process, rather than an analytic practice.

The frequency of questions we are asked about where to publish suggests a lack of collegial or useful conversation about such matters. We find that many doctoral and early career researchers are being told to aim for the top journals in their field right from the start. These are the journals that count most in audit processes and have the most prestige. We actually get quite cross when we hear of supervisors telling their students to aim for journals in which they themselves have never been published. It is of course important to be ambitious. But it is counter-productive to aim for something that is highly improbable – it is not only a waste of time but also potentially confidence-sapping. Some early career researchers *do* have the research findings and writing facilities which will garner them a top-ranking journal publication straight off, but this is not the norm. Most of us start our publishing agendas more modestly, aiming for a middle-ranking, respected journal which we know well.

This is not the only bad advice about publishing on offer. We are often told by inexperienced writers that they are about to submit a journal article that they know is not yet ready. They will benefit, they say, from the feedback they are offered. They will then write a better article because of referee comments. This is not ethical in our view. It is an abuse of the goodwill of scholars in the community who give up their time to referee. They offer their time and expertise to assist writers to improve their *best* effort, not their third best. The onus is on the writer to send in the most finished piece they can manage, not something that they know is not ready. We say more about this in the next chapter.

Our first response to the question of what journal to choose is: follow the reference. It is helpful, particularly for those who are less experienced, to check their existing reference lists to see which journals are used most. Frequent citations from one, two or three key journals suggests that these represent the discourse community within which their own research is situated.

Our other response is to say: follow the leading scholar. Looking at the websites of key figures in the field will quickly show where they are published. Their CVs will also show whether these are the scholars who are on editorial boards of journals, and they may even be editors of journals themselves. Follow the reference and follow the scholar are sensible strategies for beginning to select a relevant journal.

But we also urge people to spend more time on the processes of choice of journal. In our workshops this suggestion is often met with complaints that this is additional work. It's hard enough writing the article, we are told, without spending time on researching the journal as well.

We are reminded here of the way in which some doctoral students approach their study. They see that research equates to field work and that the first stages of their course of study is a ritual reading of literatures, rather than being the crucial work of locating their study within the field – and that this is actually the first part of the research. Similarly, we think that writing for publication is often seen as the writing itself, rather than the process of choosing a journal being a key first step, which requires time and labour, in the same way that working with literatures is a key first step in research. Stephen's story is a salutary reminder that failing to do the work at this early stage can mean that all of the rest of the time and labour spent writing the article can be for nothing.

Armed with the knowledge that the journal represents a discourse community, prospective writers clearly need to approach journal selection as an analytic process of working out the nature of the community, its histories, debates, genres, conventions, cherished truths and current hot topics.

We now offer a strategy for doing this analytic work.

Coming to terms with a journal discourse community

Our strategy for analysing the nature of a journal discourse community is comprised of four analytic questions: (1) Who is in this discourse community? (2) What does it publish? (3) What is its mission statement? (4) How does its editor see the purpose of the journal?

The fundamental stance that underpins this approach is that of critical reading. That is, information about the journal is subject to a set of critical questions which in turn lead to a 'reading' of the community and its concerns.

To illustrate how these questions might work, we use an extended example from the *International Journal of Inclusive Education*, an international peer reviewed journal published by Taylor and Francis. We selected this journal because it invites participation from a variety of disciplinary contexts – our own discipline of education, but also psychology, health and social work – and because it seeks to be both international and interdisciplinary.

We present this as a model for how to read a journal, not because we think that people should write for *this* journal. We urge readers to focus on the process that we are elaborating.

(1) Who is in this discourse community?

Most journals exist as both print and online editions. Some exist only in one form. Whichever form the journal takes, there will be information about the editor and the editorial board.

Figure 2.3 is drawn from the website of the *International Journal of Inclusive Education*. The editor and the editorial board are listed.

We made the point earlier, but it is worth repeating here, that the editor and the editorial board have been chosen because of their standing in the field.

The first question to ask of any board is: Who do you know and cite? When we show this slide, or a similar editorial list from another publication, in workshops and ask this question, some participants invariably say none or one. Our response is that if everyone is a stranger, then this journal represents a discourse community of which they are not part. If as an early career researcher they don't know any of these people, then this is not the journal to start with – or else

EDITORIAL BOARD
Roger Slee: Victoria University, Australia

Editorial Advisory Board
Mel Ainscow – University of Manchester, UK
Alison Alborz – University of Manchester, UK
Julie Allan – Institute of Education, University of Stirling, Scotland, UK
Felicity Armstrong – Institute of Education, University of London, UK
Stephen Ball – Institute of Education, University of London, UK
Suzanne Carrington – Queensland University of Technology, Australia
Tim Corcoran – University of Sheffield, UK
Bob Lingard – University of Queensland, Australia
Allan Luke – Queensland University of Technology, Australia
Meg Maguire – King's College, University of London, UK
Linda Ware – SUNY, Geneseo, USA

Figure 2.3 IJIE editorial board

they could end up like Stephen, not knowing what to say or how to behave in this environment. It is probably most sensible for early career researchers to begin with the list of journals they cite most frequently, but still go through this four-step analytic process to fine-tune their understandings and make explicit to themselves how the discourse community operates. Members of a discourse community generally know the field.

In this case, all of the scholars on the board are familiar to us either in person, or through their published work. Our next question is: What are their specialisations, what are they known for?

If we know these people, we next need to consider: What kind of work do they do? What are its characteristics? Here there is a clear connection to the kind of literature work that needs to be done in relation to any research. Researchers have to have a meta-view of the field and its key debates and figures. And it is this knowledge that they bring to the work of analysing editorial boards.

In looking at this board we would start by saying that all of the scholars, without exception, operate from a critical standpoint. While their actual research and publications span policy, progressive school improvement, disability studies, special needs and policy sociology, they share a substantive philosophical commitment to social and educational change and equity. This, then, is a discourse community which will be sceptical of articles which appear to accept the status quo. For example, policy sociologists will not accept any policy uncritically and will expect writers for the journal to do the same – to take a critical viewpoint of disability, to think about school improvement in terms of its impact on the most vulnerable groups. We could go even further than this because we know the editor has a publication which is critical of school effectiveness. We strongly suspect that uncritical articles in this field are likely to be rejected – just as journals of school effectiveness are likely to reject articles without empirically based critique.

The other thing we would say about the editorial board is not only are some editors of other journals, but some are also leading international figures in their field. This journal, then, could well be a place where significant conversations go on. In addition, published work in this journal has the potential to be taken up by people who are influential in the field because they will be reading every issue. Writing for this journal is thus entering a high-stakes conversation.

What we've done in beginning to look at this board is to sketch out some of the interests, concerns and beliefs that exist within this particular discourse community.

Some journals not only have an editorial board, they also have an editorial panel. It is helpful to look at this panel in the same way, asking the same questions. The other point to note is that an editorial panel will probably constitute a core set of reviewers. Therefore, understanding who they are and the kinds of things they are concerned about in their work will provide some clues as to how any new submission might be read and reviewed.

Figure 2.4 shows the large number of people on the IJIE editorial panel. It is helpful to see this extended panel as potential reviewers.

It is therefore useful to ask: How would X on the editorial panel respond to this new work? How would they see it connecting to or speaking to their own? It is also sensible to ask: Are there any people on the editorial panel for whom my work has particular relevance? This is a clue about which literature to include, cite and engage with in the article.

The editorial panel in Figure 2.4 also says something about what 'International' means in the title of the journal, *International Journal of Inclusive Education*. The panel consists of members from primarily English-speaking countries. It should not be concluded that the journal is only interested in articles from these countries. What is more likely to be the case is that writers will be expected to write in such a way that their article speaks to readers at least in those countries listed. Here we see there are scholars from the UK, from Australia, from the US and from a smattering of other locations. Writers for this journal therefore need to understand what is happening in policy, practice and scholarship at least in these places in order to contextualise their work and make it relevant beyond their own location.

Having established something about who is in the journal discourse community, it is then important to consider what kinds of things they are interested in.

(2) What does the journal publish?

Many books on publication suggest looking at what the journal publishes. We agree that this is very important. We suggest taking the contents lists of six or so issues of the journal and then reading the titles and abstracts carefully. Again, we will illustrate our approach through the use of an example and key questions. The point here is to continue to analyse the nature of the discourse community, and, in particular, the kinds of academic work that it supports.

We can see in Figure 2.5 that there are some 'giveaway' phrases in the titles that signal particular research paradigms. The first article by Mortier *et al.* refers to an account of different perspectives: this suggests to us that the source of the 'different perspectives' is likely to be derived either from policy analysis or research with human subjects. A discourse community insider may well understand that this title also suggests a potential for a discussion of diversity and differences from which a normative critical analysis will be derived. The second article by Reichrath *et al.* offers a 'systematic review'. We guess that this is likely to be literature-based and sits within a tradition of some kind of evidence-based

Editorial Panel:
Adrienne Alton-Lee – *Ministry of Education, New Zealand*
Michael Apple – *University of Wisconsin-Madison, USA*
Derrick Armstrong – *University of Sydney, Australia*
Andrew Azzopardi – *University of Malta, Malta*
Kalwant Bhopal – *University of Southampton, UK*
Tony Booth – *Canterbury Christ Church, University College, UK*
Barbara Cole – *Institute of Education, University of London, UK*
Bob Connell – *University of Sydney, Australia*
Joanna Deppeler – *Monash University, Australia*
Alan Dyson – *University of Newcastle, UK*
Chris Forlin – *Hong Kong Institute of Education, People's Republic of China*
Lani Florian – *University of Aberdeen, Scotland, UK*
Trevor Gale – *University of South Australia, Australia*
Rosalyn George – *Goldsmiths College, University of London, UK*
David Gillborn – *Institute of Education, University of London, UK*
Linda Graham – *University of Sydney, Australia*
Mary Kalantzis – *Royal Melbourne Institute of Technology, Australia*
Jane Kenway – *Monash University, Australia*
Tony Knight – *Victoria University of Technology, Australia*
Leith Krakouer – *Institute of Education, University of London, UK*
Colin Lankshear – *McGill University, Canada*
Levan Lim – *Nanyang Technological University, Singapore*
Missy Morton – *Canterbury University, Christchurch, New Zealand*
Sigamoney Naicker – *Republic of South Africa*
Sip Jan Pijl – *Instituut voor Orthopedagogiek, The Netherlands*
Bill Pink – *Marquette University, USA*
Sally Power – *Cardiff University, UK*
Naz Rassool – *University of Reading, UK*
Sheila Riddell – *University of Edinburgh, UK*
Kitty te Riele – *University of Technology, Sydney, Australia*
Fazal Rizvi – *University of Illinois at Urbana-Champaign, USA*
Leslie Roman – *University of British Columbia, Canada*
Robert Savage – *McGill University, Canada*
Umesh Sharma – *Monash University, Australia*
David Skidmore – *University of Bath, UK*
Tom Skrtic – *University of Kansas, USA*
Gary Thomas – *University of Birmingham, UK*
Martin Thrupp – *Institute of Education, University of London, UK*
Carol Vincent – *Institute of Education, University of London, UK*
Federico Waitoller – *Arizona State University, USA*
Gaby Weiner – *University of Edinburgh, UK*
Geoff Whitty – *Institute of Education, University of London, UK*
Lyn Yates – *University of Melbourne, Australia*

Figure 2.4 IJIE editorial panel: the potential reviewers

International Journal of Inclusive Education 14 (6), 2010

Supports for children with disabilities in regular education classrooms: an account of different perspectives in Flanders. *Kathleen Mortier, Geert Van Hove, Elisabeth De Schauwer*

Interventions in general education for students with disabilities: a systematic review. *Enid Reichrath, Luc P de Witte, Ieke Winkens*

The DSM and the dangerous school child. *Simon Bailey*

The end/s of education: complexity and the conundrum of the inclusive educational curriculum. *Deborah Osberg, Gert Biesta*

Understanding reason in policy reform: engaging 'problematic' families. *Kym Macfarlane*

Inclusion of pupils perceived as experiencing social and emotional behavioural difficulties (SEBD): affordances and constraints. *Joan Gaynor Mowat*

Figure 2.5 A sample IJIE issue with titles

study; we don't know what kind it might be from the title. The third article by Bailey refers to 'the dangerous school child' (yes, that's Simon from Chapter 1). We know that this is the kind of rhetoric that is characteristic of Foucauldian analysis. Macfarlane's article may well also come from some kind of critical discourse perspective. The last article by Mowat refers to 'affordances and constraints' in conjunction with 'inclusion' of particular students and we assume that this has a school or classroom pedagogical focus and that it may use a form of cultural historical activity theory as its basis.

This brief analysis of titles of one issue suggests that a diversity of approaches to the topic of inclusion might be characteristic of the journal. This would be encouraging, we think, to researchers worried about whether their particular approach will 'fit'. However, we can also tell something more about who is in the discourse community. We note a mix of well-known and less-known authors in the field, which suggests that early career authors are likely to be welcome.

However, we can check these hunches out further by going to actual abstracts of articles.

It is helpful to look at individual abstracts to get a deeper sense of the substantive issues that are covered, how and to what ends. We need to ask when reading an abstract: What content is covered? What debate in the field is being addressed, if any? What is the methodological approach, and what theoretical approach is used?

In Figure 2.6 we show one abstract from the IJIE journal that we are considering.

The ends of education: complexity and the conundrum of the inclusive educational curriculum

The conundrum of the inclusive educational curriculum is that the more inclusive a curriculum becomes in practice the less inclusive it becomes in principle. In this paper we explain the conundrum and argue that its appearance is a product of what could be called 'object-based' logic which is underpinned by a deterministic understanding of causality. As long as we employ object-based logic to think about curriculum, we cannot avoid asking what a curriculum is for. Whoever answers this question necessarily excludes other possibilities. We argue that a relational of 'complex' understanding of causality, which is shared by complexity theories, poststructural theories, deconstruction and Deweyian pragmatism, offers a way out of the conundrum by offering a different understanding of process and hence the guiding role of the curriculum in the educational process. In allowing the possibility of a guiding role for the curriculum, while dispensing with the need for a curricular 'end', complex logic can inform an understanding of curriculum which succeeds where humanistic education in its various forms has failed. (Osberg and Biesta, 2010)

Figure 2.6 IJIE sample abstract

We can see that this article is written from a philosophical tradition and addresses a key disciplinary concern, that of 'causes'. It is a 'think piece' (see Petre and Rugg, 2011, Chapter 7, on paper types) in that it does not refer to a specific empirical study. It canvasses a wide range of philosophical lines of thought, from pragmatism to poststructuralism, from Dewey to Derrida (deconstruction). It offers these as an approach to thinking about curriculum as process and practice, rather than as input–output (when we do something, then this will be the result). This, then, is a substantive critique of most contemporary Western national inclusion policies, and by inference, at least some of the work that has been published in the journal.

This brief analysis of this abstract tells us that this journal, perhaps unlike the one that Stephen wrote for, does not shy away from trenchant critique and potentially difficult debate. That this abstract appears at all tells us that the editor and the editorial board want to promote new and confronting ideas within the broad discourse community. Again, this should be encouraging to those who want to write something that is not necessarily 'mainstream' within the readership.

We can apply the same kind of critical reading to any number of issues of our chosen journal. To illustrate, we have undertaken this exercise by looking at issue 15(9) of IJIE, a total of ten abstracts. We show our analysis in table form (Table 2.1). The questions that guided our analysis are:

Table 2.1 Analysis of IJIE 15(9)

Article	Topics	Debates	Author position	Methods	Theory	Fit with discourse community
(1)	Deaf bilingual education in Spain	Provision of sign language, mainstreaming	Strong advocacy – 'inside' position	SWOT analysis using nominal group analysis	Not apparent	Acute needs group
(2)	Performing arts training for disabled students	What counts as success	Supportive of principles of programme researched	Case study	Not apparent	Support for the practice
(3)	Assessment practices in USA and Netherlands	Same or different goals for learning, critique of current approaches	Advocacy of 'solution-focussed' assessment	Policy analysis	A theory of assessment	Policy and practice problem
(4)	Brain-injured children thinking aloud	Mainstreaming	Advocacy	Not clear	Not clear possibly psychological?	Acute needs group
(5)	Trends in enrolments in an Australian state	Mainstream v special schools	Critical of policy	Policy analysis	Not clear	Policy problem
(6)	Inclusive classroom practice	Teacher practices	Normative critical position	Ethnography	Sociocultural activity theory	Practice problem
(7)	Teacher education in Ireland	Teacher and teacher education practices	Normative critical position	Survey and interview	Not clear	Practice problem
(8)	Indigenous girls in Queensland	Gender debates, gender and inclusion theory	Feminist critical position	Interview-based case study	Nancy Fraser on recognition and redistribution	Policy, practice and theoretical problems
(9)	Principals in Trinidad and Tobago	School efficacy	Advocacy	Survey and interview	Not clear	Practice problem
(10)	Legal framework in USA	Legal affordances	Advocacy	Document analysis	Not clear	Policy problem

(a) What topics are covered? What topics are not?

(b) What key debates are being addressed?

(c) How clearly have the authors stated their position and their argument? How bold and/or moderate have they been?

(d) What kinds of methodologies are used? What are not? Are there any obvious preferences?

(e) Is there any evidence of the theoretical resources they draw on?

(f) How congruent do these seem with what is known about the discourse community from the analysis of the editorial board?

We can see from this very broad brush analysis that:

(a) The topics cover more than special education, but encompass other 'groups' such as Indigenous girls. We can assume, therefore, that the journal takes a broad view of inclusion and does not see it as confined to disability. The topics are also international, and cover a range of foci from legal frameworks and enrolment trends to single classrooms. Thus, we can say that this is a discourse community with a wide range of interests.

(b) Many of these articles address the vexed question of mainstreaming and the physical separation of children versus variously adequate mainstreaming practices. However, the knowledge base of the profession is also at issue. We can assume, therefore, that the discourse community is broadly in favour of mainstreaming but alert to the problems with simplistic approaches.

(c) All of the authors take a stand. None is simply reporting. Their positions range from a more distantiated critical position to a strong advocacy of a particular practice, as in the assessment article. We can assume from this that there is a considerable shared commitment among this discourse community and that uncritical positioning will receive short shrift in the reviewing process.

(d) There are a range of methods used from document analysis to the standard survey and interview. The discourse community is not hostile to literature work nor is it committed to a doctrinaire qualitative–quantitative divide.

(e) Very few of the abstracts make explicit any theoretical resource and those that do are drawn from sociology and psychology. We can assume, then, that this is a discourse community which is interdisciplinary in its approaches and that referees may well be chosen on the basis of their specific disciplinary fit to the specific article.

(f) The discourse community is concerned with, and likely to share some understandings about, practice problems, groups with acute needs, and policy issues. We read into this that a writer is unlikely to have to spend a great deal of time justifying their focus per se, but rather allocate their words to outlining their particular angle and approach to a practice problem, group or policy.

It is interesting to note that this particular journal has nine issues per year and around ten articles per issue. This suggests that inclusion is both a very popular area, and also that it serves a relatively large and active discourse community which writes a lot. It is not clear whether this means there is a rapid turnover of articles, but the question of turnover is raised just by the sheer number of issues that are published annually.

(3) What is the mission statement?

Armed with the knowledge gained from the first two exercises, it is now possible to approach the journal mission statement with a view that it is a text in context (Figure 2.7). If we had approached the mission statement straight away we would have been reading the statement without knowledge of the specific discourse community, and thus might well read into it what we wanted to see. Understanding something of the journal and its concerns allows us to 'decode' its stated intentions from a more informed perspective.

A few phrases immediately strike us when we look at this mission statement. A 'strategic forum' signals that the journal editors see this as a significant site for debate about key issues in the field; 'multi-disciplinary' is repeated twice, suggesting it is highly important. Our analysis to date has helped us to see what is meant by this, and how the journal does foster multi-disciplinarity. It accomplishes this both by accepting a range of articles and having special issues which foster interdisciplinary approaches. This is not, then, an empty commitment. The definition of inclusion as based in institutions (schools, universities and technical colleges) signals the sociological basis of the journal and distinguishes it from the dominant individualised approach taken in policy and in much

---

The International Journal of Inclusive Education provides a strategic forum for international and multi-disciplinary dialogue on inclusive education for all educators and educational policy-makers concerned with the form and nature of schools, universities and technical colleges. Papers published are original, refereed, multi-disciplinary research into pedagogies, curricula, organisational structures, policy-making, administration and cultures to include all students in education. The journal does not accept enrolment in school, college or university as a measure of inclusion. The focus is on the nature of exclusion and on research, policy and practices that generate greater options for all people in education and beyond.

Figure 2.7 IJIE mission statement

educational psychology. This raises a question about the claim for multi-disciplinarity, which, as we understand from our previous analysis, is not necessarily exclusionary. We are particularly interested to see that the mission statement also contains an explicit statement about what it will not accept – articles which simply focus on access and enrolment. This degree of openness is relatively rare and we can only speculate whether it arose as a result of being bombarded with articles coming from alien discourse communities where uncritical questions of access and enrolment are in and of themselves sufficient.

There is one final source of information about journals and that is 'horse's mouth'.

(4) How does the editor see the purpose of the journal?

There are many ways of finding out what editors, in particular, think about the purpose of the journal. They appear at conferences and are accessible by email. They are also increasingly available as podcasts on publishing websites. It is, of course, important to understand that editors often speak aspirationally about what they hope for the journal and, as we saw from Stephen's story, they are not the only people who matter in deciding what gets published.

There is a podcast of the editor of IJIE, Professor Roger Slee, available on the journal homepage: http://www.tandf.co.uk/journals/IJInclusiveEd. We cannot reproduce the whole interview but have chosen a few key points from the transcript. At the beginning of his talk Roger says

> The aims of the journal are to provide a record of the developing research interests into issues of exclusion in education and how barriers are constructed for different groups of more or less vulnerable people in education. So it's looking at the development of the research agenda there.

Roger refers both to a record of what is happening in the field, but also the development of a research agenda. This is not atypical of journal editors in our experience; they often see the journal as not simply serving a discourse community but actually building and shaping it. Indeed, one of the characteristics of new areas of research is the appearance of a new journal; we can think here of the beginnings of research in ICTs and the resulting growth in journals in the field as different positions emerge and develop.

> I want to see it (the journal) become increasingly more international because that was one of the aspirations at the outset, but that's always been very difficult. We tend to get a lot of Brits, Australians and North Americans writing for the journal, that's been the preponderance of contributors and

indeed readers. More recently we have more Northern European readers and contributors. There have been more folk from Asia and from Africa writing for the journal as well and that I think is a really good thing. So to promote that is important.

Here we can see the field-shaping power that the editor does have. We saw a similar representation of international scholars from the analysis of the editorial panel, but what may be emerging in the widening of authors in the journal is an eventual widening of the geographical distribution of the discourse community. This may be reflected in future editorial panels.

> And then there's the cross-disciplinary aspiration of the journal; that it is becoming more cross-disciplinary over time and that's something that I want to continue to promote so that it's not everyone reading the journal in the same church, if you like, that it does become genuinely a forum for debate and engagement with issues.

This statement resonates with the repetition of 'multi-disciplinarity' in the mission statement, but is perhaps at odds with its sociological definition of inclusion, and our analysis of the editorial board and panel where a particular set of disciplines predominate. If reviewers come from a particular critical orientation with a strong sociological background, they may or may not be as open as the editor is to other traditions. It may well be the case that some new contributors to the journal get the kinds of reviews that are out of their frame of reference and this may be hard to accommodate. This is not an uncommon problem. However, we can see from our analysis of contents that there is a range of disciplines represented in the journal issues, suggesting a degree of editor steerage via the choice of reviewers.

Editors, of course, are not the only sources of information about journals. Other members of layer 2 – regular readers of the journal, experienced and published writers and regular reviewers – can help to make explicit the conventions and hidden assumptions of the discourse community. Conferences also often have 'Meet the editor' sessions and these again provide opportunities to hear the discourse community. The point of talking to members of the discourse community and of going to editor's sessions is to listen for the clues about layer 2 and 3, not simply to take reams of notes about how-to-write-an-article.

So what, now what?

No single source of information about a journal will in and of itself be sufficient. (See Epstein *et al.*, 2005: 59–63, for further suggestions about targeting journals.) There are inevitably tensions and contradictions in discourse communities. As we explained at the beginning of this chapter, layer 2 is heavily populated and diverse. Not everyone agrees with each other. There are discordances as well as concordances. However, it is important to come to terms with the things that are held in common. We know that developing expert knowledge about a discourse community takes time and that it can be discouraging to know you don't know enough. It is, however, part of the work of becoming a published writer and those who persevere will find that the hard work pays off. Finding the reader is the important first phase work of publication.

The process we advocate enables choice. Once the dimensions of the discourse community become apparent there is a choice to be made amongst possible journals in which to publish. Some disciplines do not have a lot of journals to choose from whereas in other areas, such as education, there are a large number of journals and communities. However, there is mileage in thinking about new journals in the field. Editors will be keen to solicit interesting work and to build the journal's reputation. Many established journals can take months to arrange refereeing and then up to two years for an accepted article to reach final publication. New journals, by contrast, can offer significantly quicker publication timelines and sometimes more support. It is helpful to keep an eye on publishers' websites to see what journals are new. There are mail shots and leaflets distributed at conferences about journals and especially new ones. These can be a very helpful source of information about opportunities to 'get in at the start'.

It is equally helpful to ask colleagues to share information about special issues, new journals, acceptance rates and publication backlogs. Most university departments contain scholars who sit on editorial boards and/or who edit journals. It is perfectly acceptable for early career researchers to ask advice from those who are more experienced members of the scholarly publication field. However, the busyness of work and the conventions of collegial interaction seem to restrict the opportunities for informal discussion about what and where to publish.

The significant point to stress is that it is important to pick the right journal. In order to decide whether this is the right journal, the prospective writer must imagine themselves as part of the discourse community they are choosing. In imagining themselves speaking, writing and debating with those who are already active in the community, there is an opportunity to ask: Does this feel right? Am I a good fit here? Do I want to be here or somewhere else?

Once this question is answered it is important to move on to consider what this particular discourse community might be interested in. What do they want and what might they be keen to read about? This is the focus of the next chapter.

Chapter 3

What's the contribution?

Assuming that the writer has now selected a journal and knows something about the specific discourse community that it supports and shapes, our next consideration is to think about what is going to be written and how. This is not simply a matter of outlining the topic and detailing headings around which the writing will be organised.

In workshops we ask, 'What's the contribution going to be?' Actually, we don't say that. Most of the time we say, 'So what? Who cares? Why write about this? What's the point?' This can be very confronting as often writers imagine that we are questioning their scholarship in a mean-spirited and denigratory way. But when we say *So what* and *Who cares* we are speaking as quasi-representatives of the discourse community in order to assist writers to imagine themselves not as mere reporters of work, but as active players in the field with something to say. Our concern is to get writers to think about and articulate what their research has to offer and to make explicit the connections between what they think they have to say, and the discourse community's concerns.

The metaphor we most often use is that of a conversation. In this chapter we explain this third key concept and why it is that we see the contribution made by an article as an offering to a conversation. We then provide a strategy – the Tiny Text – which provides a structure for the writer to articulate and plan their contribution.

The contribution

A common assumption is that the journal article always follows a research report format: aims, methods, findings, discussion, conclusion. This is sometimes known as the IMRAD structure – Introduction, Method, Report And Discuss (we address this misconception later in Chapter 6). It may be the case that this is actually how the abstract is organised. Indeed, some journals, particularly in the sciences, *require* writers to shape their abstract according to a set of given headings. For example, the *British Journal of Obstetrics and Gynaecology* requires five subheadings: Objective; Design; Participants; Results; Conclusion, while the *Journal of Affective Disorders* uses four: Objective; Method; Results; Conclusion.

Such subheads signal the report genre, and seem simply to require a description of what was done in the research. So it is not surprising that writers in these discourse communities learn to shape their texts accordingly. Although the social sciences are often less explicit in their stated requirements for a report, sometimes novice writers do assume that a 'scientific report' is required. We saw this in our analysis of Gerri's abstract at the end of Chapter 1, where she reproduced (not consciously) a three-part structure to describe her research: (1) gap in the literature, (2) findings, (3) conclusions. The result was a 'troubled text' which did not clearly articulate the contribution or what the writer was offering the field.

We suggest that it is more useful to think of the abstract as an argument – a text that makes its key point explicit and highlights its contribution to the field. Argumentation is typically thought of as a text which begins with something that arouses interest, then articulates a clearly stated issue or question, takes an explicit position, presents evidence to support this position and to refute contrary views, and concludes with an explicit restatement about the claim being made (see, for example, Bjork and Raisanen, 2010; Graf and Birkenstein, 2010).

To say that an abstract should be an argument is not to say that people cannot write report-like abstracts and articles. Certainly they do and these do get published in some journals. But it is our experience that even when journals require or expect a report genre, they still want more. They want argument. They want the point – the contribution – made explicit.

This came home to us recently when perusing abstracts from the *British Journal of Clinical Pharmacology*. In Figure 3.1, an example from one issue (65(3): 377–385), the authors have shaped their report-like abstract according to the traditional headings of their discourse community: Aim, Method, Results, Conclusion. This text appears on the right side of the page. However, we are struck by the two blocks of text on the left, immediately below the title which compete for the reader's attention. Here we find additional subheadings which are not part of the orthodox structure: 'What is already known about this subject?' and 'What this study adds'. To us these clearly mark out a move by the editor of the journal to highlight the So what: to visually and verbally make the writer's contribution tangible so the reader will be enticed to read on. While the language of the abstract remains detached and descriptive, the additional text argues the point about the value and significance of the electronic prompt:

An electronic prompt in dispensing software for a targeted clinical intervention has a significant effect on pharmacists' behaviour. A markedly increased rate of recording and performing the targeted clinical intervention was found.

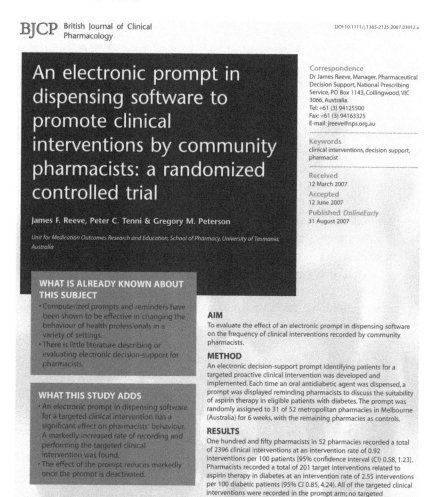

BJCP British Journal of Clinical Pharmacology

DOI:10.1111/j.1365-2125.2007.03012.x

An electronic prompt in dispensing software to promote clinical interventions by community pharmacists: a randomized controlled trial

James F. Reeve, Peter C. Tenni & Gregory M. Peterson

Unit for Medication Outcomes Research and Education, School of Pharmacy, University of Tasmania, Australia

Correspondence
Dr James Reeve, Manager, Pharmaceutical Decision Support, National Prescribing Service, PO Box 1143, Collingwood, VIC 3066, Australia.
Tel: +61 (3) 94125500
Fax: +61 (3) 94163325
E-mail: jreeve@nps.org.au

Keywords
clinical interventions, decision support, pharmacist

Received
12 March 2007
Accepted
12 June 2007
Published OnlineEarly
31 August 2007

WHAT IS ALREADY KNOWN ABOUT THIS SUBJECT
- Computerized prompts and reminders have been shown to be effective in changing the behaviour of health professionals in a variety of settings.
- There is little literature describing or evaluating electronic decision-support for pharmacists.

WHAT THIS STUDY ADDS
- An electronic prompt in dispensing software for a targeted clinical intervention has a significant effect on pharmacists' behaviour. A markedly increased rate of recording and performing the targeted clinical intervention was found.
- The effect of the prompt reduces markedly once the prompt is deactivated.

AIM
To evaluate the effect of an electronic prompt in dispensing software on the frequency of clinical interventions recorded by community pharmacists.

METHOD
An electronic decision-support prompt identifying patients for a targeted proactive clinical intervention was developed and implemented. Each time an oral antidiabetic agent was dispensed, a prompt was displayed reminding pharmacists to discuss the suitability of aspirin therapy in eligible patients with diabetes. The prompt was randomly assigned to 31 of 52 metropolitan pharmacies in Melbourne (Australia) for 6 weeks, with the remaining pharmacies as controls.

RESULTS
One hundred and fifty pharmacists in 52 pharmacies recorded a total of 2396 clinical interventions at an intervention rate of 0.92 interventions per 100 patients [95% confidence interval (CI) 0.58, 1.23]. Pharmacists recorded a total of 201 target interventions related to aspirin therapy in diabetes at an intervention rate of 2.55 interventions per 100 diabetic patients (95% CI 0.85, 4.24). All of the targeted clinical interventions were recorded in the prompt arm; no targeted interventions were recorded in the control group. The effect of the prompt decreased over the study period and was not maintained after prompt deactivation.

CONCLUSION
An electronic prompt significantly increased pharmacists' recording of the targeted clinical intervention in diabetic patients. An electronic decision-support prompt has significant potential to promote community pharmacists' contribution to the quality use of medicines.

© 2007 The Authors
Journal compilation © 2007 Blackwell Publishing Ltd

Figure 3.1 Screen shot: British Journal of Clinical Pharmacology

Thus, even in what appears to be a more traditional genre requirement in the sciences, we see a textual add-on, signalling the importance for writers of all discourse communities articulating their contribution to the field.

But what do we mean by the contribution and how is it located?

At this point in the chapter we want to engage with some of the people who populate layer 2, editors and reviewers. They are the people who judge what counts as a contribution and they do have a strong sense of what this means. We have drawn here from a set of journal editor interviews that are available on the Taylor and Francis Education Arena website (http://www.education arena.com/expertInterviews/).

For Madeleine Arnot, the editor of the *British Journal of Sociology of Education*, the contribution not only means having something to say, but something that is important to the field. The advice she offers to prospective authors is to consider not only whether the article is of interest, but whether it also adds something of significance to the discourse community.

> Ask yourself: Is your research worth publishing? Are you at a stage where you have sufficiently identified what is original about it? All knowledge is in some senses worth publishing but it has to be developed enough to be published. It has to have an original idea in it, perhaps one or two ideas that are clearly expressed and their originality is visible to the readers. It's worth publishing if it moves thinking forward, if it moves the boundaries of knowledge forward.

Here we get a notion of a contribution as knowledge that has value – it moves thinking forward. It has the potential to change thinking in the field. After we have read the paper we know more than we did before. It reduces our ignorance (Wagner, 1993). It does not duplicate or repeat something that is already well known. Nor is it a simple description. It is self-conscious about what it adds to the field and the community, in the way that the breakout boxes in the pharmacology journal in Figure 3.1 demonstrate very clearly.

But how does the writer identify their contribution? David Gillborn, editor of *Race and Ethnicity in Education*, suggests that a paper with a contribution will be one which presents only one or two ideas.

> We really need the author to know what their point is. In lots of papers it's like the author hasn't really made their mind up, they've got three, sometimes four ideas and they're not quite sure whether the paper's about all of them or none of them. I think the strongest papers usually have one point to make and they make that point powerfully, with evidence, and they locate it within the field. Very often I'll get really interesting papers

but they're not quite sure what they're saying and often those things just need to be started again because they're so disorganised that it's difficult to give clear advice on how you can change that. You know, you really need to sit down and work out what it is you're trying to say.

We agree. In our workshops one of the most common problems we see stems from the writer's lack of clarity about the point of the article. As a result, the argument that is being made is unclear, the article goes nowhere and there is no powerful concluding section which makes explicit what is new to the field.

Gillborn recommends one strategy for finding the point. It begins with identifying the reader, that is, thinking about the discourse community for whom the article is being written, and to whom the argument will be relevant, interesting and instructive.

I often, with students and with authors, suggest that they think, 'Who's the person I want to read this? Who am I addressing?' Whether it's an activist group in the community, the leading researcher in your field, someone who you want to give you a job. Imagine who that person is and then imagine that you've walked into an elevator at a conference or wherever, that person is in the elevator and the doors shut. You've got ninety seconds with that person before they get out of the elevator. What do you want to tell them about your research? You can't tell them everything about it, you can't, you know, spend three days telling them about the intricacies of French philosophy and how it relates to what you've just done. You've got ninety seconds; you need to work out what's important about your work that you can give someone in ninety seconds.

It sounds silly, it sounds deceptively simple but actually most people that are writing, they'll be writing up research that's taken a year, two, sometimes three years or more. Trying to actually distil that down into something that makes sense quickly is a really hard job and it's much better that you do it before you write rather than sitting down and starting with the first page and then seeing where it goes. Because that's where you wind up with those lengthy articles that never really get to a point, that just kind of talk around issues.

This is a helpful suggestion and it is one worth practising in the bathroom or bedroom prior to sitting down to plan a paper. An alternative imagination-based strategy is to imagine how the paper will be written about in a literature review. If someone was to read the article and then write about it in one sentence, how would they describe its content and its point? Both of these exercises – the elevator and the literature review – require the writer to think about themselves as presenting their ideas to a real reader who will have a response to what is being said. Those responses can be anticipated through these imaginings and the point of the article clarified and refined so that it can be simply and quickly expressed.

While these two imagination-based exercises seem straightforward, we find in workshops that some people resist imagining. They are reluctant to discipline themselves to a few short sentences or less. 'But you need to have read. . .', they say, 'You can't understand this without really understanding the context.' Well, yes and no. The point of the exercise is not to duplicate the actual article, but to use a creative approach to find the memorable, original and singular addition to the scholarly discourse community.

We want to point here again to the importance of the imagination. We began Chapter 1 by noting that imagination was a vital part of identity work/text work. In Chapter 2 we argued that it was important to be able to imagine the scholarly self as part of a discourse community. And it has appeared again here, this time in imagining speaking with a representative of the scholarly community or being spoken about by them.

Now we ask for not only imagining a reader, but beginning a dialogue with them.

The conversation

We have just referred to a contribution as adding knowledge to a discourse community. We need to clarify what we mean by adding. It is common to think of knowledge as a set of things, to which each article adds another thing. Or to imagine knowledge as pile after pile of articles. This is not a very helpful metaphor because it suggests that knowledge is somehow fixed and more like a material object than anything else. But if we think of knowledge as being a social construction then it never actually sits outside of human activity and is always in formation (see Thomson and Walker, 2010, for an elaboration of this argument). Even when that activity resides in an artifact such as a book or paper, it is actually something that has been made, and then needs to be remade by every reader (Fish, 1980). The act of writing is a process of making meaning, but the material article, the words on paper, has no meaning in its own right. The words only become meaningful when they are read and interpreted by readers. The act of reading is, in fact, to enter into a dialogue with the text, bringing what is on the page into conversation with our own experiences. The act of writing is an act of anticipation – it is to create a text which will stimulate a conversation with the reader. Writing is thus the beginning of a dialogue and a process of interactive meaning-making.

If the writer invites conversation through their journal article, and the reader enters that conversation through their reading, and then responds in their own piece of writing, we can begin to see how journals make possible conversation via articles. And if we understand that both the readers and writers around a journal belong to a particular discourse community, we can see how the conversation constitutes a social dialogue. We can thus think of the journal itself as an ongoing set of conversations between writers and readers in a scholarly discourse community. And if each article makes a contribution, then the conversation in the journal can be seen as a collaborative process of knowledge building.

The reason we have said it is important to know the debates and key figures in the field is so that the writer enters the journal discourse community as an informed participant – knowing the unsettled questions, prior knowledges, shared understandings and common languages. The implication of this understanding – that an article is a conversation in 'occupied territory' (Kamler and Thomson, 2006) – is to emphasise that the writer cannot, must not, assume that there has never been any discussion about the topic beforehand.

The writer therefore needs to *situate* their work in the context of the journal and its discourse community. They must pay attention to who has written about their topic before. Stephen Ball, editor of the *Journal of Education Policy*, is unequivocal in stating the consequences of failing to understand the nature of the journal discourse community, its concerns and its ongoing conversations.

> Some people who send papers make two very common mistakes. One is they simply send it to the wrong journal and that's becoming increasingly the case . . . it's surprising how many people submit papers clearly never having read the journal, never opened a page of the journal or read on the website what it is the journal's interested in. And increasingly, as the Managing Editor, I'm fielding papers at the initial stage which we would never send out for review and I write back and I say sorry, this doesn't fit within the remit of our journal.

According to Ball, then, one risk of failing to understand the interests of the journal discourse community – and to demonstrate that failing in the text – is the increased likelihood that the paper will never be sent out for refereeing. The un-situated paper falls at the first hurdle. But that's not the only pitfall, according to Ball.

> Related to that, the second common mistake is people who want to publish papers in areas that we are interested in without ever referring to previous papers in the same area that we've published in the journal, which is a silly

thing to do really. If you want to publish a paper on issues around school choice in Australia, or wherever, a paper on school choice – I don't know, we must have published over the 20-odd years of the journal 20 to 30 papers on issues around school choice in different ways. To not refer to any of those in your submission to the journal is just foolish, really. But it's not simply foolish, it's also failing, I think, to engage in a scholarly process of cumulation of knowledge, cumulation of theoretical develop-ment, cumulation of understanding.

Ball stresses the need for writers to articulate their contribution in light of the ongoing knowledge producing conversation in the journal. He goes on to note that the process of not making the fit and the conversation clear is wasteful of everyone's time.

It can be frustrating as an editor. I feel I'm having my time wasted when people send papers to the journal which patently don't fit in the journal at all. And they're wasting their own time because then they have to wait for us to read the paper and look at it and send it back to them and then they have to go through it again. I imagine there are some people who spend their life sending their papers to journals that don't want to publish them, not because they're not good papers but because they're just in the wrong place.

So I think one of the key things for anybody who wants to be published in this journal, as in any journal, is to, you know, read it. Even if you don't bring yourself to actually read the papers from beginning to end then look through the issues, look through the sorts of things that are being published, look through the contents list, look for other papers that have been written around the area, in the field that you're trying to write about and then draw on those.

This seems common sense, but we are often shocked in workshops, and as reviewers, by how often people don't seem to get this. As an editor of the journal *Educational Action Research*, Pat is surprised at how many articles she receives which are not discussing action research. These never make it to review. Like Stephen Ball, Pat and her colleague editors just send the articles back with a polite note telling the writers to find the right journal next time.

Equally often, both of us have had the experience of reviewing articles which fail to 'read' the discourse community. Some time ago Pat had to review an article from a teacher education journal. It originated from Eastern Europe. It described the way in which teacher education was moving away from a highly didactic, centralised approach to one that promoted teacher reflection. The article concluded that teacher reflection was a Good Thing. The difficulty with this argument was that for the journal in question this was hardly new news. There were already shelves of articles published on the topic in this and other teacher education journals which the writer had ignored. And the potentially interesting contribution – the take up of Western models of teacher education and how they worked in this Eastern European context – was ignored. Instead, the message that was delivered was one which was of significance to the audience in the home country, where reflective practice was new news. The journal's discourse community, by contrast, would have been much more interested in finding out what was happening in the Eastern European country.

The last point we want to make about the contribution, therefore, is that it must address the So what question. Each article needs to be self-conscious about the point it is making. The So what should be explicitly addressed in both the beginning and the conclusion of the article and argued throughout. The reader should be left in no doubt as to why this particular insertion into the conversation matters and why. We spend the remainder of this chapter and the next two on strategies for how this can be achieved.

To summarise what we have argued to date, we conclude with some questions to orient the writer to the task of conversing with the specific discourse community:

- What is the journal?
- Who is the reader?
- What is the contribution I want to make to the conversation in this journal?
- Why is this an issue, and to whom, and why?
- What might happen differently if my contribution is taken up?

While the prospective writer may not be able to fully answer these questions, they are a helpful orientation to the task to come.

A strategy: Tiny Texts

Abstracts are often overlooked and left until last. They are seen as a tiresome necessity, something that journals require but which can be put off until the very last moment. Titles get much more of a writer's time than the abstract. In a time when many readers decide whether to click past the title *and* the abstract and actually download the article, this myopic attitude is no longer viable.

Since we first began working on abstracts (Kamler and Thomson, 2004), we have come to understand their potential to inform the reader, and before them the reviewers and editor, not only about what has been done, but to also engage the writer in the text work/identity work which is critical to academic writing.

We initially began to take a formal interest in abstracts because we were interested in the advice journals were giving to writers. We found that this advice was generally vague and confined to specifying word length or a set of subheadings from the report genre (see IMRAD at the beginning of this chapter). In our analysis of abstracts from ten social science journals, we were surprised to find considerable variation in their formulation, but a uniform lack of specific information about why the article was written, and what it was offering. This gave little incentive to a reader to bother going any further.

We now regard writing abstracts as a critical strategy for clarifying the contribution and not only finding but also taking a place in the conversation. In a good abstract the writer speaks with authority, not simply describing or reporting what will be in the article, but delineating their case and specifying their particular point of view. In other words, in writing the abstract the writer makes themselves both an active participant in the field and a legitimate member of the discourse community. They are not reporting to examiners, or describing an innovative practice to their line managers or funders. Nor are they simply presenting an advertisement for the article to come. They are performing themselves as a scholar (albeit in formation) with something significant to say, with a perspective and a defensible base from which to speak. This may feel like a bluff. The writer may have to write themselves as more certain than they feel, but it is this move to textualise the scholarly self with an authoritative stance which creates a more confident scholar.

We do a lot of work with workshop participants on what we call Tiny Texts. We call abstracts Tiny Texts because they are relatively short in length, but high in practical yield. The intellectual and emotional labour involved in crafting a persuasive Tiny Text is invisible work, yet readers immediately recognise a 'good one' when they stumble across it. David Gillborn, editor of *Race and Ethnicity in Education*, makes this point pithily.

> A good abstract will tell you what the key issue that's addressed is, it'll give you an idea of the methods that have been used and the conclusions that have been arrived at. So that abstract ought to tell someone whether it's worth them spending part of their life reading this paper. If the abstract doesn't do that the chances are the paper will have further weaknesses.

As reviewers we agree completely. A poor abstract bodes poorly for the article that follows. We therefore always recommend that after writers have done the work of researching the journal and its scholarly community, they move next to an abstract, rather than a plan, or just writing. We know that some people like to 'just write' and write and write. That's fine. That's one approach, but not ours. We offer a strategy and invite readers to try it out for themselves. In workshops we find that working with Tiny Texts – writing abstracts, talking them over, analysing their structure and rewriting – and rewriting – is profoundly generative.

We offer a core strategy of four textual moves, and two variations on the core strategy which are designed to suit particular kinds of papers, the empirical article for a method-focused journal and a theoretical contribution.

Four moves

We think of an abstract as having four moves. We call these Locate, Focus, Report and Argue. We show these four moves in Figure 3.2.

LOCATE: this means placing the paper in the context of the discourse community and the field in general. Larger issues and debates are named and potentially problematised. In naming the location, the writer is creating a warrant for their contribution and its significance, as well as informing an international community of its relevance outside of its specific place of origin.

FOCUS: this means identifying the particular questions, issues or kinds of problems that the paper will explore, examine and/or investigate.

REPORT: this means outlining the research, sample, method of analysis in order to assure readers that the paper is credible and trustworthy, as well as the major findings that are pertinent to the argument to be made.

ARGUE: this means opening out the specific argument through offering an analysis. This will move beyond description and may well include a theorisation in order to explain findings. It may offer speculations, but will always have a point of view and take a stance. It returns to the opening Locate in order to demonstrate the specific contribution that was promised at the outset. It answers the 'So what?' and the 'Now what?' questions.

Figure 3.2 The four moves of a Tiny Text

We now show an example of these four moves as they apply to one of our own abstracts (Abstract 3.1) from the *Educational Researcher*.

The failure of dissertation advice books: towards alternative pedagogies for doctoral writing

LOCATE: Anxious doctoral researchers can now call on a proliferation of advice books telling them how to produce their dissertations. While these might be helpful in the short term they offer little that the doctoral researcher can use to analyse their own texts or to understand the source of their anxieties.

FOCUS: This article reveals some characteristics of the self-help genre through a textual analysis of a corpus of published books, delineating their key genre characteristics.

REPORT: Our analysis shows that the texts: produce an expert–novice relationship with readers; reduce the dissertation to a series of steps; claim to reveal hidden rules; and assert a mix of certainty and fear to position readers 'correctly'.

ARGUE: We argue for a more complex view of doctoral writing as both text work-identity work and as a discursive social practice. We reject transmission pedagogies that normalise the power-saturated relations of protégée/master and point to alternative pedagogical approaches that positions doctoral researchers as colleagues engaged in a shared, common, unequal and changing practice.

(adapted from Kamler and Thomson, 2008)

Abstract 3.1 Four moves in a published paper

In the Locate we have identified an issue and suggested that it is problematic and, by inference, that we have a different view. Given this, we offer a specific Focus which is designed to allow us to say something about the problem we have identified. In Report we detail the four findings that have resulted from our analysis. In Argue we offer a theoretical framework and on the basis of this propose a course of action. The title clearly signals our critique in the word *failure* and our contribution in the phrase *alternative pedagogies*.

What goes in the four moves varies in length and complexity. Sometimes the article is situated in a field where there is considerable debate and the writer needs to state their position quite clearly. So sometimes the Locate work, for example, will be more descriptive and sometimes more argumentative. Some arguments might lead to more than one conclusion. Some may provide a challenge to existing thinking, a new lens on the problem(s) or a potential implication for a more general issue. These are categories of moves, not recipes for how much to say about what.

Five moves

Recently we have experimented with a more scaffolded version of the four moves, particularly for writers who want to enter a discourse community where there is a strong focus on methodology. We added an additional category – that of Anchor to follow Focus – in order to separate out a clear and succinct description of methods from the Report of the findings. Abstract 3.2 shows these five moves as they apply to one of Pat's abstracts (Thomson, 2011).

Creative leadership: a new category or more of the same?

LOCATE: New categories of leadership are continually being invented. Because the ways we think are productive of the ways in which we act, it is important to hold these rhetorical innovations to account.

FOCUS: This paper focuses on the latest of the leadership categories – creative leadership.

ANCHOR: Mobilising a Foucauldian notion of 'discourse' I deconstruct the notion of creative leadership as it has recently been represented in five published texts.

REPORT: I suggest that the interpretation on offer has a determinist view of the future, ignores the history of debates about creativity, offers creativity as a generic skill and underestimates what it is that teachers and leaders might need to do in order to work creatively. I show that the notion of creative leadership on offer is strongly connected with that of creative learning, and put the 'recipe' offered by one set of texts into conversation with a body of empirical evidence about what is happening in schools that aim to promote creative learning.

ARGUE: I argue that what is evident from the dialogue between the texts and the empirical studies is that it is pedagogical leadership that is absent but is actually most required, embedded in leadership/management principles and practices that promote social justice.

(Thomson, 2011)

Abstract 3.2 Five moves in a published paper

In Abstract 3.2, the separation out of the Anchor, the term intended to indicate the foundations on which the report is made, ensures that the writer makes a specific statement about the empirical work that has been done. In this case, it is relatively short; in larger studies this might extend to two or three sentences. Some journals are particularly anxious about ensuring that methodology and methods are made explicit in both the article and the abstract, and the addition of this Anchor move achieves that end.

Three moves

Another variation we are currently working with is a reduction from four to three moves. This change was a response to the demand by workshop participants for a framing that would support more theoretically oriented papers. In this version, Focus and Report are replaced by Problematise, which is in reality an exploration of the issues outlined in Locate. The example in Abstract 3.3 from *Nurse Education Today* illustrates these three moves.

Writing up and writing as: rediscovering nursing scholarship

LOCATE: Nursing is a relatively young academic discipline which only moved en masse into the higher education sector in many countries during the 1990s. Perhaps in a bid to enhance and accelerate its credibility, the nursing academy has embraced the values and practices of evidence-based medicine and the associated 'gold-standard' experimental research paradigm as its dominant discourse.

PROBLEMATISE: Empirical scientific research has become the most valued and highly rewarded activity for nurse academics to pursue, and the tenets and standards of research have come to define the entire academic project of nursing. As a result, there has been a gradual shift from nursing as an academic discipline founded on scholarship to one based on research. Research is no longer seen as merely one aspect of the scholarly work expected of an academic, and is now often regarded as the main (and sometimes the only) activity necessary to gain promotion.

ARGUE: I argue in this paper for a more positive view of scholarship; indeed, that scholarly activity is both the foundation and the creative driver of the academy. I suggest that the 'gold-standard' academic output of the research report is restricted in the contribution it is able to make

---

to the development of the discipline of nursing, and that a far broader and more critical academic base is required. Whilst empirical research supplies the basic building blocks of the discipline, it is critical and creative scholarship that provides the plans and designs that turn these piles of bricks into useful structures.

(Rolfe, 2009)

Abstract 3.3 Three moves in a published paper

In this abstract the Locate is a description of a current situation, giving background and context to the issue. The Problematise is evaluative and makes claims about a serious shortcoming within the field. This is a kind of meta-analysis offering a bird's eye view of a trend in an entire field. Argue provides the opportunity for the writer to suggest an alternative approach which is grounded in an explicit philosophical position, the practical implications of this are indicated. This kind of article can be seen as a form of professing where a problem in the field is identified and an argument is made for a new, and better direction.

In offering this abstract it is important to recall Stephen's experience which we described in Chapter 2. He chose to make a critical intervention in a discourse community which was hostile to such an activity. In Abstract 3.3 we can assume that the discourse community in this journal was receptive to internal debate. We note that the writer, Gary Rolfe, says that nurse education is a young discipline and this may have something to do with its willingness to entertain articles which examine the field itself.

We can safely assume that in the article Rolfe is able to offer evidence of his engagement with the breadth and depth of literatures in the field and that this is the basis for his argument. However, on the basis of the abstract alone, readers would not be surprised to find out that the writer was beyond early career status. Rolfe certainly writes as if he is an experienced and senior figure in the field, and indeed when we googled him, we discovered that he was a professor of nursing. We note that it is always more possible for senior members of the field to write these kinds of critiques because of their in-depth knowledge of the discourse community and its histories, debates and concerns. Furthermore, when the article is published the discourse community sees it not simply as an upstart contribution, but emanating from deep engagement and commitment, an 'insider' contribution.

Understanding the discourse community through analysis of their abstracts

Tiny Texts are helpful, we have suggested, to clarify the contribution that is to be made to a particular discourse community, and to get the line of argument sorted out. There is, however, another way in which they can be used: to analyse existing abstracts written by other scholars.

In workshops we often use the four moves of the abstract as an analytic tool to discern common ways of writing in the discourse community. When we use the moves in this way, we find that many abstracts do not include all of the moves we have suggested. In fact, it is the Locate and the Argue which tend to be missed out, either one or both. Abstract 3.4 from the field of finance and economics is a case in point.

Long-run stockholder consumption risk and asset returns

LOCATE:

FOCUS: We provide new evidence on the success of long-run risks in asset pricing by focusing on the risks borne by stockholders.

REPORT: Exploiting micro-level household consumption data, we show that long-run stockholder consumption risk better captures cross-sectional variation in average asset returns than aggregate or non-stockholder consumption risk, and implies more plausible risk aversion estimates. We find that risk aversion around 10 can match observed risk premia for the wealthiest stockholders across sets of test assets that include the 25 Fama and French portfolios, the market portfolio, bond portfolios, and the entire cross-section of stocks.

ARGUE:

(Malloy *et al.*, 2009)

Abstract 3.4 Different discourse communities have different conventions

Abstract 3.4 is an assertion of a contribution to the field in the form of new evidence. Clearly the reader needs to bring their own understandings of the Locate work which is not stated. Readers are assumed to know the extant literatures to which this article provides something new. In fact, the Report quite clearly offers a comparison between the model proposed here and the existing approach. The reader is also left to come to their own conclusions about what might happen as a result of this offering to the field.

However, when workshop participants engaged in an analysis of this abstract, they suggested that writers in the field of finance rarely made their arguments explicit. This raises the question of convention and whether the mores used by particular discourse communities are fixed and inviolable or are to some extent malleable and open to change. One question to ask is, would an article which puts in a Locate and Argue be rejected by a journal in this discourse community or might it improve taken-for-granted practices?

The four moves offer the possibility of interrogating the writing practices of discourse communities. We think that it is advantageous to all writers in any discipline to experiment with the Tiny Text structure and use the moves for analyses, because by making the conventions explicit, writers are better able to make choices. We therefore reframe these moves in Figure 3.3 as a set of questions that can guide the analysis of abstracts – those written by ourselves and others in the discourse community.

- How well is the work **located** in relation to broader discipline/policy/ practice issues/problems? Does it address the concerns of the discourse community of the selected journal?
- Has the abstract **focused** the topic of the paper and identified the kind of research that was undertaken? Is the focus clearly related to the more general problem or issue of concern to the discourse community?
- Does the abstract **report** the research that was undertaken, its methods and design? Does it make the findings/evidence accessible to a broader readership and provide the key to the argument that follows?
- What is the **argument**? Is the 'So what?' question addressed? If not, what might it be? If yes, can it be made stronger? Is there also a 'Now what?'

Considering the whole text: Are the four moves coherent? Are there connections between each of them? Is there a discernible link between Locate and Argue?

Figure 3.3 Questions for analysing the moves

Getting started

It is always helpful to use an abstract to work out what needs to be said. However, there are times when writers just get stuck. For us, there is no point in the four or five move Tiny Text strategy if the writer just ends up staring at the heading LOCATE for far too long. In these kinds of situations, we suggest that one way to get unstuck is to use some sentence beginnings to get the thought processes going.

LOCATE: . . . is now a significant issue (in/for) . . . because . . . (Expand by up to one sentence if necessary)

FOCUS: In this paper I focus on . . .

ANCHOR: The paper draws on (I draw on) findings from a study of . . . which used . . . in order to show that . . . (expand through additional sentences)

REPORT: The analysis of the findings shows that . . .

ARGUE: The paper argues that . . . and concludes (I conclude) by suggesting that . . .

Figure 3.4 Some sentence beginnings to get unstuck

We offer one set of beginnings (Figure 3.4) for the five move abstract which can be used to get the thought processes going.

We don't see the sentences in Figure 3.4 as a formula and we certainly don't imagine that readers of this book are going to send abstracts that sound like this to their journals of choice. Nothing could be further from the way in which we imagine this strategy being used. No, this is not a default. Once the argument becomes clearer, the writer can then get rid of these starters and go back to a three, four or five move Tiny Text which is bespoke to the argument.

So what, now what?

This chapter has focused on the notion of the contribution as an offering to an ongoing conversation in a specific discourse community. We provided a number of variations on the Tiny Text theme. We hope that readers will experiment with them as a way of starting to think about their own work. We argued that it is the Locate and Argue moves in the abstract that do the work of delineating the contribution. An abstract that omits these moves could be considered to be exclusionary since it assumes prior knowledge that only insiders are likely to possess. Alternatively, it signals a paper in trouble.

However, this is not the end of the Tiny Text. The next chapter analyses the work that goes on when writing and revising abstracts, and the kinds of struggles that writers experience when working through the four moves.

Chapter 4

So what? Who cares?

Writers are always in process, never arrived, finished and polished. Early career writers come from a variety of contexts – some are engaged in doctoral work, some are recently completed, some are working as jobbing contract researchers, others are practitioners whose continuing concern is the conduct of teaching and learning. Writers often struggle to move from these positions with their habituated ways of thinking, speaking and writing to a new position – that of the authoritative scholarly journal writer.

We've written elsewhere about the doctoral graduate still writing for their examiners, still believing they have to demonstrate that they have read everything and know everything (Thomson and Kamler, 2010). Part of the struggle to write an effective abstract and article is re-imagining oneself as a new scholarly self. In this chapter we provide further examples of how this struggle for identity appears on the page.

This chapter brings together our three key concepts: text work/identity work, discourse community and making a contribution as a conversation, and shows how these play out in writing abstracts. We look here at the abstract texts of early career writers – both the first drafts they brought to our workshops and the ones they revised and later submitted to journals. We examine the struggles they experienced and worked with to become more authoritative writers for their designated target journals.

Our aim is to show the difficulties, movement and progression that writers experience as they use the set of abstract moves to help them articulate the So what of their work. This is what we mean by the somewhat confronting title of this chapter: 'So what? Who cares?' We saw at the end of Chapter 3 that abstracts which do not spell out an argument rely entirely on the readers to make the connections to broader contexts and the existing literature. In most discourse communities this is not good enough. A journal article is expected to do more than report. It must make explicit its contribution. So what is a shorthand way of saying, 'What is the point and why bother reading?'

Titles are also an important textual strategy which help the writer crunch the So what and we conclude this chapter with a brief discussion of this even tinier text – its possibilities and dilemmas. We begin, however, with five struggles in the writing of early career researchers. These are: (1) drowning in detail, (2) trying to say it all, (3) writing without a reader in mind, (4) struggling to find the angle, and (5) worried about being 'out there'. These struggles demonstrate that it is not a straightforward matter to follow our four or five abstract moves and simply fill in the blanks. What is always involved is the politics of identity work and negotiating the discourse communities we come from and those we wish to be read by. We hope that readers will find these examples of use as they work with their own Tiny Texts.

Drowning in detail

Dorothy is in the final year of her PhD and both she and her supervisor are somewhat anxious about her completing. Dorothy was asked by her supervisor to use the five move abstract to think about a possible paper from one of her draft thesis chapters. Her supervisor thought that this pedagogic intervention might be a way of improving the chapter, as well as producing a publication which would be helpful to Dorothy as she tried to find work in a university. Because Dorothy lives some way from the campus, the abstract was to be sent to the supervisor by email.

Here is what she sent (Abstract 4.1). Dorothy has used all of the five moves but appears to be submerged in superfluous verbiage.

Why headteachers leave Anglican primary schools

LOCATE: The departure of headteachers in primary schools in England is defined as being the result of a demographic 'time-bomb' of baby boomers, headteachers leaving due to age or retirement. The 'doability' of the role with its increasing accountability and performativity and possible resulting stress and workload are cited as contributing factors. Almost a quarter of primary schools in England are Anglican but the body of literature about leadership in Anglican schools is small compared to that about Catholic schools, the majority of which has been conducted in the UK, USA and Australia.

FOCUS: By sampling headteachers in Anglican schools this study contributes to that body of literature.

ANCHOR: This paper is drawn from a doctoral study which investigated why headteachers leave a post and/or the profession and where they 'go to'. A mixed method study established the future 'destinations' of headteachers of Anglican primary schools in England and explored their reflections on their decision to leave a post. 156 headteachers participated in the national survey and forty-eight headteachers were interviewed.

REPORT: This paper argues that there is an unrecognised group of headteachers leaving headship whose destinations and reasons for leaving are not reflected in the literature about supply and retention, the focus of which is often on the departure of 'baby boomers' and on solutions to supply such as succession planning. The paper also highlights evidence/data that suggests that a significant number of headteachers going to a subsequent headship are leaving Anglican schools for non-Anglican schools and argues that this has implications for dioceses in their response to the 'time-bomb' of departing headteachers and the shortage of applicants for church school headships often highlighted by annual surveys into the labour market (Howson). This paper explores factors that contribute to the decision to leave of headteachers in both groups. In doing so it contributes to existing knowledge about the 'doability' of the role, stress and workload and accountability and performativity. Thematic analysis of survey and interview data show that these factors include 'external' expectations, additional accountabilities related to Anglican school headship and 'internal' expectations related to identity and experience.

ARGUE: The paper suggests that relationality may be the key to recruitment and retention within the Anglican sector.

Abstract 4.1 Dorothy drowns in detail

The imbalance of writing between the sections shows where Dorothy is drowning – in the Locate and in the Report. She knows a lot about the background to her study – faith schools and the departure of headteachers – which she describes in great detail. Dorothy *does* attempt to create a warrant for her research by noting that there is not a lot of literature related to Anglican schools. Her Anchor is the clearest writing in the abstract. We can see that in Report she proliferates details as a list. Readers are not clear which of this information is important or whether any is more important than any other. Even though she uses the terms 'highlight' and 'argue', this is not what we read. The abstract assumes an insider appreciation of the problem and its possible solutions and is not well organised for anyone outside of the study. Dorothy does, however, have a sense of what the contribution might be which she states as being related to the 'doability' of the job.

The way in which Dorothy conceives Focus and Argue really pinpoints her struggle. While she clearly knows the study, its methodology and findings, she doesn't know how to elaborate these for an article. A Focus which says the writer will contribute to the literature can mean anything. Similarly, the one-sentence Argue offers a minimal statement and it is not clear how it follows from the Report or what it means.

When Dorothy's supervisor received the abstract by email, she could see what the problems were. Too much detail. Too little focus. No sense of a reader. No So what! She decided to rewrite the abstract using what she could of Dorothy's words. Her aim was to model the kind of writing required by the targeted journal discourse community, and to make propositions for further conversation about what actually could be said and argued on the basis of Dorothy's data and analysis. In this rewrite (Abstract 4.2) the italics signal what was kept from Dorothy's original text.

Why headteachers leave Anglican primary schools

LOCATE: Policy makers and scholars agree that there is a serious problem in the recruitment and retention of headteachers. Studies show the problem to be a complex mix of a *demographic 'time-bomb' of baby boomers – headteachers leaving due to age or retirement –* and *the 'doability' of the role – increasing accountability and performativity* resulting in *stress and workload.* While surveys in England suggest that there is a particular problem for Anglican schools, there is to date little research which investigates whether their faith base has anything to do with apparent difficulties in attracting and keeping school leaders. Given that Anglican primary schools constitute a quarter of all English primary schools, this is perhaps surprising.

FOCUS: This paper examines why Anglican primary headteachers leave a post and/or the profession and where they 'go to'.

ANCHOR: *156 headteachers participated in* a *national survey* conducted around vacancies advertised during one calendar year; *forty-eight headteachers were interviewed.* In addition to seeking information about career trajectories and working conditions and patterns, the study *established the future 'destinations'* of participants, all of whom were in the process of leaving their post.

REPORT: *Thematic analysis of survey and interview data* show that, in addition to the kinds of issues generally found in supply research, faith was a significant issue for many heads. Heads refereed to *'external' expectations, additional accountabilities related to Anglican school headship and 'internal' expectations related to identity and experience.*

DOROTHY, I'M NOT CLEAR HOW THE ARGUMENT GOES. . . HERE'S ONE I MADE UP. . ..

IMAGINED ADDITIONAL REPORT: However these responses did not follow a neat geographical pattern; heads in the same diocese for example could have very different experiences and responses and this was in part due to the local context, but also due to their own spiritual orientations.

IMAGINED ADDITIONAL ARGUE: This diversity means that it may be difficult to find adequate policy responses to this supply problem; indeed, the evidence from the research suggests strongly that a generalised solution across the country or even across a single diocese may well fail. Rather, it seems that *relationality*, that is the ways in which site-specific, individual head, governor and diocesan relationships are established and maintained, *may be the key to recruitment and retention within the Anglican sector.*

Abstract 4.2 Supervisor revisions to Dorothy's abstract

The rewritten Locate is still long but is now argumentative rather than descriptive. It situates Dorothy's research in the broader problem of recruitment and retention. This will allow her to later make a connection to her incipient argument and the contribution that the study will make to the larger debate. The Locate work problematises the issue of recruitment and retention and creates a warrant for the study in both practice and in research. The Focus utilises Dorothy's words, but offers a sharper statement of what the paper will do. The revised Anchor is a more succinct, precise and informative statement about the study. It also offers some of the categories which were used in data analysis – career trajectories and working conditions. The supervisor wanted to emphasise that the study had a strong empirical base, something Dorothy seemed reluctant or unable to do.

The Report has been drastically reduced in order to highlight the key issue – faith – rather than list all the findings as if they were of equal value. However, the supervisor felt that there wasn't enough in the Report to make an argument. She added information that she knew about the study in order to highlight the pattern of findings. As for the Argue, the supervisor was very clear that there wasn't one. As she wasn't clear what Dorothy wanted to say, she made a provisional offering which they could then discuss. She also modelled the identity work of a confident scholar in putting forward a claim and an angle that could make the contribution to the field that Dorothy imagined.

We don't underestimate the difficulty of freeing oneself from the detail to see and to articulate an argument. We do see that the abstract structure has the potential to force the writer to engage with what they can argue, even before they know what this is. They can try out options, interact with others about what they've written, in order to gain clarity and courage. The text work/ identity work between Dorothy and her supervisor became the pivot for further rewriting and clarifying. In the end Dorothy presented the paper at a conference, but has yet to do the additional work required to bring it to publication standard.

Trying to say it all

Maria recently finished her PhD, a monograph written in her mother tongue. She is now faced with the task of turning her PhD into articles written in English. She attended a workshop with a draft paper for which she had written this abstract (Abstract 4.3). The abstract captures the kinds of problems she had in writing the paper. These are common for scholars making the transition from the thesis to the article. We call this trying to say it all, or saying everything at once.

The activity of 'writing for learning' – methodological and analytical challenges

LOCATE: Students write at all levels of Higher Education, both for the purpose of learning and assessment. This article focuses on writing for learning.

FOCUS: I will suggest methodological approaches to study how the activity of writing unfolds in different kinds of practice; and analytical approaches to the ways in which students unpack and interpret the institutional tasks they are given.

ANCHOR: The paper offers a dialogical perspective, drawing especially on theories developed by Mikhail Bakhtin, James Wertsch and Per Linell. Language is regarded as emergent, multiform, negotiated in the process, meaningful in the uptake, accomplishing social acts. Writing in educational contexts accomplishes and mediates student learning, but how can these processes be conceptualised and analysed from a dialogical perspective? An empirical case study, investigating the writing of portfolio assignments in a nursing program will be used for the purpose of illustrating the points made.

REPORT:

ARGUE:

Abstract 4.3 Maria tries to say everything

Of the five possible moves used in an abstract, here we see there is no Report and no Argue. The Locate is minimal but signals the territory – higher education, writing for learning. The absence of any other commentary gives the feeling that no one has done any work in this field and that there are no issues with which the writer will be in dialogue. But it is in Focus that the trouble really occurs. There are two major frameworks offered: methodological and analytical. These are really the foundations for a thesis rather than an article. Either one of these would be quite sufficient for a paper, provided that the Locate designated that there was a need to have a new methodological or analytic approach. Because there was no problem articulated in the Locate it is not clear why the reader needs to consider new methodological or analytic approaches. The most information is offered in Anchor, which offers yet another focus for the article – a theoretical discussion. We now have signposts to the literature review and the methodology chapters from the thesis. Finally, in Anchor we are also told an empirical case study will be presented, presumably from one of the findings chapters of the thesis. The absence of Report makes it clear that the writer does not know what the article is about. She is clearly well versed in the study and how she did it, but she cannot find a way to carve out one big idea from which she can make an argument and an article.

Maria did not revise this abstract. She started again after a long conversation about which of these ideas she might make the focus of a new article.

Like Maria, many graduated doctors attempt to compress their thesis into one article. Some do succeed in doing so, but some are tortured by the process and it severely damages their transition to published journal writer. A major challenge for all PhD gradates in the social sciences is to map out a series of articles from the thesis and segment the big book into sharply focused articles that don't try to say it all. Developing a publishing plan is something that can be done in the period between thesis submission and examination. It doesn't hurt to start on the process before the results are in and it can help to avoid the post-PhD slump/loss/grieving/refocussing. (We say more about publication planning strategies in Chapter 9.) We have observed that doctoral writers with a plan find it easier to write the first article when the others are already outlined. It frees them to narrow the focus, while being assured that critical information from the thesis will be argued elsewhere.

Writing without a reader in mind

Carl brought his co-authored abstract on assessment to a writing workshop where he was listed as first author. In fact, his co-author had greater expertise in assessment and Carl had little emotional investment in the text. They had originally written the abstract for a conference on assessment and Carl was trying to convert it into an article. But he told the workshop group he was keen to get it done quickly, so he could move on to the next article he really wanted to write. In this sense he seemed to be saving himself for a future text and had given little thought to which journal he was writing for. This ambivalence and no sense of readership appear in his abstract (Abstract 4.4) as an incapacity to specify the research and its implications.

The impact of ongoing classroom-based assessment within university English Pathway Programs

LOCATE:

FOCUS: This paper examines the effect of continuous classroom-based assessment upon teaching and learning within a university English Pathway Program (EPP). As successful completion of the program determines whether students meet the English language entry requirements for university, this constitutes a high-stakes assessment context, which typically favour standardised, summative approaches to testing, such as IELTS and TOFEL.

REPORT: Following a brief overview of the relationship between formative and summative assessment and the role of classroom-based assessment within the teaching/learning/assessment cycle, we outline the research design for this study, discuss main themes to emerge from a case study of teacher practice within one such context, and then conclude with a summary of key findings and their implications for classroom-based assessment within similar high-stakes settings.

ARGUE:

Abstract 4.4 Carl does not know his reader

Applying the four moves to the abstract quickly shows the problem. There is no Locate and no Argue. And the Report is more like an outline, a promise of what the reader will find in the paper if they decide to go further. This kind of prospective bid for what will come is not uncommon and we have found it in a number of journals and disciplines. In this sense Carl may well be following common practice in the field, generally. The phrase 'a summary of key findings and their implications for classroom-based assessment' is such an open statement, it can mean anything. The Focus is more informative. It identifies and provides background to the topic of the paper. The term 'high-stakes' appears in both Focus and Report and so it seems to be an important concept, but it is left to carry the weight of convincing the reader without giving any reasons why.

In the workshop Carl engaged with others to analyse his abstract and draft paper. His key insight was not only that he had omitted Locate and Argue, but that he hadn't adequately considered the So what for a readership who might be interested in this work. A discussion about international students in higher education, their increased market value and the problems experienced in Australian universities was what excited him. As he believed the EPP program he researched was innovative in this context, he decided to rewrite the abstract for a specific journal, *Studies in Higher Education*. Imagining a new article for this discourse community reinvigorated Carl and his revised abstract shows greater assurance and clarity because he could answer the question: Who is the reader?

Continuous assessment frameworks within university English Pathway Programs: realizing formative assessment within high-stakes contexts

LOCATE: Universities have become increasingly reliant upon English Pathway Programs (EPPs) to expand enrolments of international students who otherwise fail to satisfy standard entry requirements, as determined by standardized tests of language proficiency such as IELTS and TOEFL. EPPs provide foundation programs for mainstream university courses, with particular attention to the language skills required for academic study.

FOCUS: This article contributes to the work on alternative assessment within higher education by focusing on the use of classroom-based assessment within such programs and the formative potential of continuous assessment frameworks in the context of higher education.

REPORT: We report on an Australian case study of teacher practice within one EPP, in which ongoing classroom-based assessment contributed towards 70% of the students' final score.

ARGUE: We argue that there is significant value for using continuous, classroom-based assessment, but the high-stakes nature of higher education restricts how its formative potential is realized in practice. We identify implications for promoting more positive learning gains, including the need to re-balance assessment tasks within course structures and the value of greater teacher autonomy.

Abstract 4.5 Carl's revised abstract and title

The revised abstract (Abstract 4.5) has changed considerably. So too has the title – from a focus on classroom-based assessment (a local problem) to assessment frameworks and how these are shaped in high-stakes contexts (a more global problem). There is now a Locate and Argue and these work well to situate the paper within the specific higher education discourse community. The Locate situates EPPS within universities and identifies a problem – the recruitment and success of international students, a concern of great import in higher education in a number of countries. In fact, the repetition of 'higher education' and 'university' in all four abstract moves shows Carl being a bit overzealous to ensure he now targets his readership. Focus is reduced to one sentence which hits the contribution and delineates what the paper will do. This is a great improvement. But Report suggests a continuing problem, as the one sentence offers nothing by way of findings. Potentially, the reader needs more information about the case study as the foundation on which Carl can make his argument. Argue does, however, hint that while the findings were generally positive, there were some problems in implementation. In particular, Carl now articulates how the high-stakes context restricts the potential of continuous assessment – whereas previously he was not able to do this. He also identifies two areas for improvement, thus projecting a clearer and more authoritative stance than the 'readerless' abstract he began with.

Struggling to find the angle

Sylvia is a mid-career researcher in social work who brought this abstract (Abstract 4.6) to a three-day writing retreat. She had conducted government-funded research on youth detention and had recently completed the project report. Her key finding was framed in relation to the project brief – identifying a 'trajectory' for youth detention. Although she tries to shift the report into a research article, the term 'trajectory' still frames the title and abstract.

Fragile pathways: the trajectory from children's services to youth detention

LOCATE: Trajectories that identify risk factors and enable prediction of offending patterns are well documented in the criminology literature, yet the factors that influence the pathway from children's services to youth detention has, to date, not been documented.

FOCUS: This article uses a sociological model of a trajectory to under-stand the experiences of young people who have a dual status between child protection and youth justice.

REPORT: We report on research that identified a five-stage trajectory that begins with the initial notification to Children's Services and ends with incarceration in Youth Detention. Case files, held by Children's Services, of six young people in detention who had previously been in care were analysed. These case files contain thousands of case notes, departmental reports, assessments, emails, school reports and health records that provide a window into the day to day lives of these young people over many years. Despite different individual circumstances, this analysis identified clear patterns of events that were common to all the young people.

ARGUE: Knowledge of this trajectory reinforces the need for early intervention and points to the fact that opportunities for effective intervention become less, and more difficult, as children progress through the trajectory towards youth detention.

Abstract 4.6 Sylvia cannot find the angle

Sylvia's abstract includes all four moves and these are adequately developed for a report. That is, they take up a descriptive rather than an argumentative stance. The word *trajectory* is used not only in the title, but in the Locate, Focus, Report and Argue. The repetition signals visible constraints posed by the terms of the research grant and an inability at this point in time to move beyond these. Sylvia's team investigated a trajectory of youth detention as it had not been investigated previously, and they did appear to come up with something new. But a report for funders and an article for a journal discourse community require the writer to take a very different discursive stance, something Sylvia has not yet done here.

Thus her Locate has the appearance of a problematisation, showing that there is a gap in the criminology literature that will be addressed. For a report it is sufficient to fill that knowledge gap by reporting the findings. But for a journal article the writer needs to indicate a So what – why it is a problem, for whom it is a problem and why this matters. Focus articulates an analytic construct, the sociological model of a trajectory, but Sylvia seems to confuse the trajectory for everything else. The problem is the trajectory. The focus is the trajectory. The reported findings are the trajectory. And the argument is the trajectory. As such it feels tautologous: the abstract begins and ends with the trajectory. It is almost as if Sylvia is reporting on the research question (what is the trajectory), rather than on the problem the research was intended to illuminate.

Report is more informative and identifies five stages, using the data well and delineating the common patterns of events that were found. But Argue is really a recommendation for a report. In other words, it's a Now what without the So what. The identity work required to shift the abstract from a report to an argument is significant and difficult to do.

The discussion of Sylvia's abstract at the retreat, however, helped her to articulate an argument beyond the constraints of the trajectory. Her excitement centred on the fact that it was possible to intervene in this problem of youth detention – that social workers could make a difference *if* they knew when and how to intervene. Sylvia worked for a full day on her rewrite, which now provides a new problematisation.

Critical junctures: a model for effective social work interaction

LOCATE: Children placed in out-of-home care are at increased risk of entering the youth justice system. These are the children who from an early age are reported to authorities for child abuse and neglect, often frequently. When placement breaks down, they experience homelessness, non-completion of education, unsafe living conditions and criminal activities. Despite thousands of hours spent by social workers generating thousands of file notes, high levels of documentation do not currently produce better outcomes for this group of children.

FOCUS: This article develops a model that moves beyond documenting social problems to identifying critical junctures where intervention can make a difference.

REPORT: It reports on research which examined the files of six children who had experiences of both the child protection and youth justice systems. These files included case notes, departmental reports, assessments, emails, school reports and health records that provide a window into the day to day lives of these young people over many years. Despite individual differences, our analysis identified a trajectory comprising five stages or 'critical junctures' where the action taken by case managers can redirect the progression away from detention and towards more positive outcomes.

ARGUE: We argue that this critical juncture trajectory provides a productive framework for practice that increases the capacity for effective social work interactions.

Abstract 4.7 Sylvia's revised abstract

In the revised abstract (Abstract 4.7), Sylvia locates the problem for which the research found an answer. This is immediately evident in the new title which talks of critical junctures – rather than trajectories – and makes an explicit offer: an effective intervention model. The Locate pulls no punches. It focuses on the problem of at-risk kids, the massive amount of work being done by social workers and the ineffective outcomes. The Focus is crystal clear. A new model for intervention is being offered to the field. The Report provides more specific information about the research method and its major finding. There is a new elaboration of what a five-stage trajectory is and how it might be used. The Argue is brief, but it offers a clear contribution to knowledge and to practice.

This is a huge difference from the first abstract. Sylvia has not only shifted the genre – from description to argument – but her identity stance as well. This involved not simply changing words or getting clearer, but finding a new angle – a new problematisation for the work of the article. She was assisted by writing at a retreat where there was continued dialogue about her work.

One of the problems of writing about abstract work in a book like this is that we can't reproduce the dialogue that is often critical to the process of revision. For example, we often ask people to think of the journal article as an answer – and we ask, 'What is the problem for which this is an answer? For whom is this a problem and why? Who cares?' Then in conversation we think about how these answers can be turned into a Locate, the angle, the beginning of the article. For the readers of this book, in the absence of a formal workshop, we suggest asking these questions of oneself or meeting with colleagues to ask one another.

Worried about being 'out there'

Elaine is an academic in a business school. She is a mid-career researcher who is working hard to build a publication record. Her abstract stems from research which investigated accidents in the temporary agency workforce. Elaine knew the field and the literature well, but her struggle was to distinguish the specific contribution of her research. She brought this abstract (Abstract 4.8) to a workshop designed to increase authority in business and management journal writing.

Workplace injuries and temporary agency workers: explaining their higher risk of injury

LOCATE: Temporary agency workers have a higher risk of workplace injuries, yet few studies have identified factors contributing to their higher risk.

FOCUS: This article examines the experience of injured temporary agency workers in Australia, and draws upon the pressure, disorganization and regulatory failure model to explain their higher rate of injury.

REPORT: Quantitative and qualitative data supports the analysis. Critical factors identified include insecure employment, lack of workplace familiarity and task experience, inadequate training, and a lack of regulatory compliance by agency and host employers.

ARGUE: Recommendations centre upon the need for regulators to develop enhanced protection in both employment and occupational health and safety which is tailored to the unit and is a unique characteristic of triangular employment.

Abstract 4.8 Elaine lacks authority

Elaine has written an articulate first abstract which suggests strong understanding of her findings and their implications. She includes all four abstract moves. Yet when we look more closely at each move her struggle becomes clear. Locate consists of one sentence. She has identified a gap in the literature but has not connected this to an explanation; it is not clear why it matters that this gap exists or to whom. The Focus is clear and promises a regulatory failure model. It seems to us that there might be more of a claim here, if this is the first time that data about Australian workers' experiences has been produced. If that is the case, then this is an understatement. Report contains a minimal statement of method and an impressive list of causes for the higher rate of injury. Argue is a Now what, rather than a So what. Elaine is concerned to draw implications for the workplace and to designate reforms for occupational health and safety. We do not understand the term 'triangular employment', the last word of the abstract, and we hope the discourse community does. However, we see no connection between the Now what and the Locate. The Locate needed to go on to explain that there was a problem in practice arising from the gap in knowledge.

Elaine engaged in small group discussion using the four move strategy to analyse her abstract. In conversation she realised that her key contribution might be methodological. This energised her because it offered a tangible way to make a mark in the field. We can see how this impulse was inserted into her revised abstract (Abstract 4.9).

Temporary agency workers and workplace injury – looking beyond employment insecurity

LOCATE: International studies have confirmed temporary agency workers experience a higher risk of workplace injury than other employees. Explanations for their vulnerability, however, have been impeded by methodological constraints which contribute to the experience of hetero-geneous groups of precarious employees being analysed together, obscuring important differences amongst them.

FOCUS: This article reports on a study which addressed these constraints through multi-methods which enabled in-depth examination of temporary agency workers' employment and injury experience.

REPORT: The qualitative data from that study is reported here. The analysis confirmed that agency workers' risks derived from employment insecurity, but were compounded by factors unique to temporary agency operations, including workplace unfamiliarity, inappropriate placements, and lack of compliance by agency employers and hosts with employment and safety regulations. Temporary agency workers' risk of injury is distinguishable from other precarious employees because of the com-petitive pressures and evasion of legal responsibilities which shape the nature of temporary agency arrangements.

ARGUE:

Abstract 4.9 Elaine's revised abstract

Elaine's Locate is now more specific about the gap in the literatures. It is not just that there is a lack of work in the area, but that the explanations offered are impeded by methodological constraints. We guess that this is an argument which 'feels' more scholarly and offers an opportunity for new identity work. Elaine has the opportunity to make a contribution which is wider than this piece of work and which has more general application to other research in her field.

The Locate prepares well for the Focus. It makes a methodological claim, in that it uses a methodological term – mixed methods – and a promise of in-depth examination from the point of view of the worker. Our earlier hunch that work from the temporary worker perspective is largely lacking in the field is confirmed, although Elaine makes no mention here of Australian workers. We assume that dropping the site indicates that this is now the site of an analysis of a more widespread phenomena. In both the Locate and the Focus there is a ratcheting up of scale. Report is also more detailed and we can see the connections with the Locate work which identifies the need for a more differentiated approach to research. Indeed, the use of the terms 'competitive pressures' and 'legal evasions' make it clear that Elaine has a critique to make which her use of more differentiated methods has allowed. However, she includes no Argue move and has not yet made an explicit argument. She needs to go back to Locate and state clearly that it is the methods she used which produced this new finding. She needs to assert the practical difference that these findings will make and the potential for new regulatory frames, based on her findings, to significantly reduce temporary worker injury.

Her titles, in fact, show this shift. Elaine has moved from an explanation in the first draft ('explaining their higher risk of injury') to a bid for making a new and important contribution in the second ('looking beyond employment security') and moving beyond the common sense of the field. The abstract text does not yet go as far as it might in asserting a significant critique and contribution. It does not yet have the authority of a senior commentator in the discourse community. We would like to imagine Elaine out in front of her discourse community wagging her finger and saying: 'You've got it wrong. Your research practices are obliterating the problem and the responsibility for things that are going wrong. People are being hurt because we have not understood the problem well enough. I've got a better way'. This is what we mean by identity work and getting authoritative. Note that in this image we have moved Elaine out of the elevator – David Gillborn's suggestion for locating the contribution (see Chapter 3) – to standing on a soapbox talking to the field.

To conclude, we briefly consider the power of the title to further assert or pinpoint the contribution.

Crunching the title

Even when the abstract is sorted – or we think it is sorted – it is helpful to reduce the point of the article even further, to less than a sentence which contains the most essential element. It's the contribution that needs to be highlighted and potentially, if it's important, the method or place or sample. This is what we mean by crunching the title. Nailing it. The title is an even tinier text than the abstract, but it does a great deal of work.

It is now more important than ever to have searchable titles that will be picked up on the internet by a wide array of readers. The clever title is probably amusing to the writer and the two other people who bother to read the abstract. However, a myriad of others have passed it over because they haven't got a clue what it's about. At best, an adroit pun or a riveting quote can only make half a title. The other half needs to leave the fickle browser in no doubt about what they are choosing. It could even be said, in the case of titles in the age of online publication, that boring and factual is good.

It was for this reason that we titled one article 'The failure of dissertation advice books: Towards alternative pedagogies for doctoral writing' (Kamler and Thomson, 2008). Not very exciting and you can bet we'd thought of others. The first part of the title, before the colon, articulates our argument quite strongly (failure); the second part suggests we are offering something different (alternative pedagogies for doctoral writing). This is an unambiguous bid for the contribution we wish to make, albeit still modest (towards).

In his discussion of what makes a good title, Hartley emphasises the need to attract, inform *and* be accurate. 'It needs to stand out in some way from the other thousands of titles that compete for the reader's attention, but it also needs to tell the reader what the paper is about' (Hartley, 2008: 23). Hartley categorises thirteen different types of title, each with advantages and disadvantages (23–25). These range from titles that announce the general subject or emphasise the methodology to those that attract by alliteration or using puns. He also reports on Soler's (2007) examination of 570 titles in biological and social science articles, which distinguishes four types:

- full sentence constructions, for example 'Learning induces a CDC2-related protein kinase';
- nominal group constructions, for example 'Acute liver failure caused by diffuse hepatic melanoma infiltration';
- compound constructions (i.e. divided into two parts, mainly by a colon), for example 'Romanian nominalizations: Case and aspectual structure'; and
- question constructions, for example 'Does the Flynn effect affect IQ scores of students classified as learning disabled?'.

(Hartley, 2008: 26)

Soler's analysis showed that the most popular type of construction in both the social sciences and sciences was the nominal group type, while questions were rarely used. The full sentence construction occurred only in the sciences while the compound colon type appeared mostly in the social sciences.

But the key issue, we think, is that a title (whatever its syntactic construction) can at the outset help crystallise an idea for both the reader and the writer. As the abstract is revised, the title also needs to be checked to make sure it signals whatever shift has been made. This was the case for Carl, Sylvia and Elaine. As they changed what they understood they wanted to say, to whom and why, they also had to change their titles.

So, for example, consider the change in Carl's titles as he moved from abstract to abstract:

Draft 1: The impact of ongoing classroom-based assessment within university English Pathways Programs

Draft 2: Continuous assessment frameworks within university English Pathway Programs: realizing formative assessment within high-stakes contexts

The constant terms in both drafts are *assessment*, which is the topic, and *English Pathways Programs* which is the object of Carl's research. But the relative position of these change as Carl gets clearer about his journal readership. So, in the first draft the focus is the EPP and how it is assessed. This signals a local evaluation. In the second draft a two-part colon structure appears. Assessment in EPP Programs is placed before the colon, but a change is signalled by the term *frameworks*. It is the broader frameworks used in universities, rather than a specific program, which Carl is putting forward for consideration. After the colon he adds *within high-stakes contexts* to signal his new argument. The changes are slight, perhaps, but were critical to Carl clarifying his point of view for a specific higher education readership.

We often find in workshops that when a group of writers become familiar with one another's evolving drafts and arguments, they can suggest more effective titles than the author. This kind of intervention can be particularly useful when the writer is still unclear or diffident to name their contribution. This was the case for Ellen, a mid-career researcher in child and maternal health, who told us she was surprised that her research had not been taken up more widely in her field. An analysis of one of her titles suggests a reluctance to make her argument explicit to her discourse community:

Maternal alcohol consumption and diet, and initiation and duration of breastfeeding: Data from the longitudinal study of Australian children

This title uses the two-part compound structure, but its most obvious feature is that it is descriptive and additive. It names a number of topics that have been drawn from Ellen's longitudinal study, but there is no attitude or stance. Nothing is highlighted or made prominent; just added together with a string of *ands*. Barbara suggested an alternate title to better capture Ellen's argument:

Maternal diet and breastfeeding: A case for rethinking physiological explanations for breastfeeding determinants

The key move here is from description to argument. The focus is sharpened in the first part of the title to two topics only: diet and breastfeeding. The second part is more assertive. The word *case* signals an argument will be made based on the data; while *rethinking* makes a critique and a claim simultaneously.

Ellen was happy with this alternate title and adopted it, in consultation with her co-author, to whom she wrote after the workshop:

> What do you think? This is what I was saying to people when I was explaining the poster at conferences last year – but I don't think we've argued our point strongly enough here. This makes it a much more interesting paper and links it to our previous smoking and obesity work (and intention).

This kind of work on titles is worth the effort, for titles speak loudly and start the process of reader anticipation. When revising titles we can ask: How well does the title signal my desired discourse community? How assertively does it signal the contribution I want to make? How will it signal in an online search the major point I am making and to whom?

So what, now what?

We've addressed five different kinds of abstract troubles that writers in our workshops present. We know that if they went ahead and wrote their paper using the thinking apparent in their abstracts, the resulting papers would all have been deeply flawed – and highly unlikely to make it through a refereeing process. We've illustrated how working on these Tiny Texts can position the writers and their actual writing much more positively.

It's more efficient and effective, we think, to sort out fuzzy thinking through a small piece of prose rather than spending a good chunk of time writing and rewriting a whole paper. Of course, having crunched the title and sharpened the abstract, the article still needs to actually be written.

We get onto that now. Our next move is what we call beginning work.

Chapter 5

Beginning work

We know how hard it is to find time to write. Despite all of the pressure to write, doing the writing is always balanced against teaching responsibilities, our duties to students and what seems like an unending stream of meetings and administrivia. We don't recommend it, but we have found ourselves writing on weekends and in early mornings in order to keep up with the *amount* that we need to write, let alone read enough to position *what* it is that we want to write. In a sense this is the way that things are now done in the academy.

And getting started is the worst. The screen is blank and, it seems, so is the mind. It is not uncommon for us, and we know for others, to make several false starts. It is hard to see the white page as full of possibility. It too often seems to signify an absence and a lack in us.

This chapter offers some strategies for dealing with the empty screen and the terrors of the blank page. We have already introduced the Tiny Text and put it to use as both a development and diagnostic tool. In this chapter we want to use it as a planning tool to support the process of writing in either sustained and/or in more on-off time spans. We then go on to discuss strategies for beginning the writing: CARS (creating a research space), OARS (occupying a research space) and sentence skeletons – modelling writing on the texts of more expert scholars. We encourage readers to not only read but also to experiment with these strategies *and* to modify them to suit themselves and the specific writing tasks that they are undertaking.

The Tiny Text as a planning tool

It is not always possible to find three days to do a first draft of an article. In fact, doing this is the exception rather than the norm. So most of us start something and then, on returning to it a few days or weeks later, find it hard to remember where we were up to. What was that paragraph referring to? Why on earth that sentence? We must have had something in mind when we wrote that, but who can recall now! The answer to finding the time to write is not to simply reduce the time so that one writes in shorter bursts. We know that other writers recommend writing in small pieces and not trying to write everything at once. However, our experience is that without some kind of plan to guide this activity, small pieces of writing can be the equivalent of wandering around a strange city trying to find the hotel. We might luck out and stumble across it but we might not. The difference is that in writing, there is no friendly policeman to ask for directions. We are on our own. Having the equivalent of a map is therefore very helpful in order to avoid wasting precious time.

Writing in shorter bursts requires organisation. If we don't have the luxury of weeks to sort out a text – that is, to learn what the argument is through the writing and rewriting process (and who does?) – then it is vital to do some of this learning ahead of time. We advocate the use of an abstract, which becomes the map to stop us losing our sense of direction. In fact, regardless of the time we have, we propose that the abstract can be a *very* useful planning tool.

We want to demonstrate how the abstract can be used as the first move in constructing the actual text. Abstract 5.1 is from a published article by Pat and her colleague Helen Gunter (2008). We have divided it up into a five move abstract: this is in fact how it was written.

Researching bullying with students: a lens on everyday life in an 'innovative school'

LOCATE: Bullying is a serious problem in schools.

FOCUS: This paper reports on a project in which the authors worked with a group of secondary students in an innovative school in the north of England to research issues of bullying and safety.

ANCHOR: The student researchers used photographs to stimulate conversations with focus groups of their peers.

REPORT: The data showed that while there was little serious bullying in the school, there was an everyday practice of name-calling, isolation, and physical hassling associated with the formation and maintenance of a hierarchy of sub-cultural groupings in the school.

ARGUE: The students' research not only challenges the notion of bullying as necessarily involving a perpetrator and victim, but also offers a lens through which to examine the imbrication of educational differentiation via setting, testing and choice with youth identification practices. It is suggested that this project also has implications for the ways in which one understands and works for inclusion.

(Thomson and Gunter, 2008)

Abstract 5.1 Abstract for use as a planning tool

The first action to be taken from this abstract is not to start writing. The first thing to do is to decide, on the basis of this abstract, how many words need to be allocated to each section. This is an extremely helpful exercise because:

(1) it forces us to go to the journal to check for the required word length and then plan how to write just that many words

One of the complaints of journal editors is that people don't stick to word lengths, so it is a good idea to try to do this. No more and no less. The editors' concern is not simply a sign of some kind of control-freak behaviour. Rather, it is that publishers (layer 3) limit the pages of journals to the size that they think they can make profitable. One of the jobs that editors and editorial boards must do is to think about how many articles they want to publish in each issue, and therefore what word length is both possible and desirable. They must balance the needs of the scholarly discourse community to read a balanced and persuasive article and to read a range of articles in a single issue, against the commercial requirements that come with editorial territory.

(2) it makes us think about the weightings of various sections

As referees, we often come across articles where most of the words have been used up in the first part of the paper, so by the time we reach the end the argument and the conclusion are truncated. The article is top-heavy – all literature and report and no argument to speak of. As such, the top-heavy article fails to make the case for its contribution and it is likely to be rejected or the writer asked to do some pretty major revisions. So, it's important to make sure that there are enough words left at the end to persuade the reader of the importance of the study. In Figure 5.1 we have mapped the word lengths for Abstract 5.1 and put planning notes next to each section of the abstract.

LOCATE: Bullying is a serious problem in schools.	Introduction located in current national and international policy context (500 words)
FOCUS: This paper reports on a project in which the authors worked with a group of secondary students in an innovative school in the north of England to research issues of bullying and safety.	Expand to 100 words
ANCHOR: The student researchers used photographs to stimulate conversations with focus groups of their peers.	Description of the site of study (500 words) Account of methodology – trigger photographs located in the visual research literatures (1,000 words)
REPORT: The data showed that while there was little serious bullying in the school, there was an everyday practice of name-calling, isolation, and physical hassling associated with the formation and maintenance of a hierarchy of sub-cultural groupings in the school.	Report of major findings – description of thematised findings moving to analysis (2,000 words)
ARGUE: The students' research not only challenges the notion of bullying as necessarily involving a perpetrator and victim, but also offers a lens through which to examine the imbrication of educational differentiation via setting, testing and choice with youth identification practices. It is suggested that this project also has implications for the ways in which one understands and works for inclusion.	Theorisation of inclusion, reference to broader literatures on school sorting and selecting (1,000 words)
Argument about the significance of the findings, viz. disjuncture with prevailing policy approach	Elaboration of some implications for research and practice (1,500 words)

Figure 5.1 The abstract becomes the road map

(3) it allows us to assign times to the various parts of the paper

The abstract in Figure 5.1 is divided into seven writing tasks. Some are bigger than others, but none is likely to take more than a solid day's work and most will take less than this. Each piece can be written as a separate and discrete 'chunk'. We know, therefore, that we need seven bits of writing time in order to complete a first draft. We also know how the argument goes because the abstract works to keep us on track. We don't lose sight of where we are going, even if we have to take weeks between sections, because we have a road map in front of us. Finally

(4) we can use the abstract to rework our ideas as we go along.

As we write we sometimes find that we start to say something different than we had originally planned in the abstract. This is perfectly normal and nothing to worry about. It happens because writing is thinking, and as we work with our data we may well see things that we weren't aware of at the start. If this happens, it is helpful to go back and rework the abstract and the word lengths. The abstract becomes an iterative planning document which clarifies how the argument goes. It helps us to be coherent and logical. So, rather than give up the abstract if there is a change of direction, the abstract tool can be easily adjusted and adapted to manage the change.

Once a plan for the paper has been developed, there is still the problem of that pesky empty screen. The introduction still needs to be actually written.

Creating a Research Space (CARS)

We have found that the strategy known as CARS (Create a Research Space) is helpful in getting clear about the work that the introduction must do. Getting clear is preparatory to writing those first few sentences.

We argued in Chapter 3 that every journal abstract needs to start with locational work. This is also the specific requirement of an introduction. The locational work in the introduction must first establish the warrant for the paper in either policy, practice and/or scholarship. The warrant, or mandate as it is sometimes called, is a statement which provides a rationale for a particular contribution to knowledge. Second, the introduction must also explain how the paper will address the issue, and indicate how the argument in the article will proceed. The introduction thus not only establishes the need for the paper, but also makes it clear that if the reader engages with the paper they will find the answer to the question or problem that has been identified.

We came across the CARS strategy as it has been elaborated by John Swales (1990). It's a heuristic based on an analysis of social science journal articles which showed the general characteristics of introductions. Swales and Feak (2004) have subsequently suggested that the notion of a *space* gives the impression of a gap, a great yawning hole which the author promises to fill. They note that this is an exaggeration of what is generally possible, which is more like, they propose, finding a *niche*. They also suggest that CARS may support a more antagonistic stance which is unacceptable in 'softer' disciplines, in small discourse communities and non-Anglophone cultures. Despite these reservations, we think that the idea of a space *or* niche, and creating the mandate for the work by elaborating the niche, sits well with our notion of locating the writer in the scholarly territory. We therefore offer it as a way of thinking about the content of that very important and frustrating introduction.

CARS consists of three sets of moves.

Move 1: Establish a territory in which the work is located

The paper must outline the centrality of the topic in a current policy, practice and/or scholarly debate, problem, or issue. This is accomplished first of all by naming the topic, and then offering some uncontentious generalisations about it. Reference to the state of extant literatures, knowledge and/or commonsense and/or policy assumptions are then briefly given.

Here is an example of Move 1, with details omitted, applied to the task of writing an introduction.

> Most scholars have at one time or another struggled with how to begin an article . . . (add details).
>
> There is a plethora of advice available on blogs, in books and in courses on academic writing. They generally acknowledge problems with writing the introduction by saying . . . (add details).

Move 2: Establish a niche for the paper

The paper must then go on to specify what it will do. This might be by way of a counter claim in relation to policy, practice or the extant literatures. It might be an indication of some contradictory views in policy or in practice. It might be the identification of a blind spot in the literatures. It might indicate where and how a different perspective and/or new knowledge might be helpful/is needed. It might offer a new theoretical take or simply raise questions to which there have hitherto been no satisfactory answers. It might suggest that the paper will continue a promising line of inquiry, or contribute to a particular tradition of research or writing. In establishing the niche, the introduction foreshadows the contribution that the article will make.

Here we continue with our writing example to show how a niche can be established.

> However, research continues to indicate that introductions remain problematic to many prospective writers. It seems that finding a way to provide assistance to the writing of introductions is problematic. This paper offers new insights into the ongoing introduction conundrum.

Move 3: Fill the niche that has been constructed

In the final section of the introduction, the writer must outline what they will do now that they have established that something needs to be done. This may be in the form of a simple outline of a research project which gives the reader some basic information about its scope and nature. It might be a description of the theoretical approach which will be explicated. In the case of a literature-based article, it could indicate the various categories of literatures which will be analysed.

This final section of the introduction concludes by indicating the key points or findings that will be made, and the shape of the article to come. (We say more about this kind of signposting in Chapter 6.)

Our example thus finishes with the outline and signposts.

> We report on a five-year series of workshops during which we developed four key strategies for writing introductions. These were . . . (add details).

> We firstly elaborate on the kinds of workshops we ran, then address each strategy in turn. We conclude by suggesting that . . . (add details). We begin, however, by outlining the theoretical underpinnings of our work.

CARS is, as we have shown, a strategy which supports a think-then-write approach to the introduction. It may well be that some writers would prefer to brainstorm on paper the things that need to go in each move. These mind maps must then be ordered and made into a set of guiding points which can be turned into prose.

Swales and Feak (2004: 244) also develop an alternative approach to CARS. This takes a more conversational approach, which they suggest is writing in order to attract an audience. Their alternative to CARS includes three steps:

- establish credibility, by sharing knowledge, justifying the need for the research and offering interesting thoughts,
- offer a line of inquiry, by discussing current problems and/or expressing interest in an emerging topic,
- introduce the topic of the paper.

They describe this approach as being suited to a 'kinder, gentler, more research relaxed world in which there is less competition for research space' (244). While we concur with this political intent and we like the notion of attracting a readership, we do think that most early writers in the social sciences are likely to be better served by using a more structured CARS approach, since they are, in reality, competing to get into print and to adopt the appropriate authoritative stance. (To this end, see Swales and Feak, 2009, on the production of abstracts.)

Focusing on the terror of the white screen and trying to craft the perfect beginning is a recipe for continued frustration and inaction for many people. We think that getting the body of stuff that has to go into the introduction up on the screen is more important than wrestling with any opening sentence. It is better to opt for CARS in order to make a start to a first draft. Creating the niche and the warrant for the research and getting a sense of the way the article will proceed is preferable to a perfect opening gambit. Stunning first sentences can wait until later. (And then, see Sword, 2012, on stylish academic writing.)

Occupying a Research Space (OARS)

While CARS does critical work in helping the writer locate their contribution – defining the space and territory – it does not guarantee that the writer knows how to put themselves in the space. The introduction is a significant place for identity work and hitting the contribution. Here the writer needs to establish their identity as a researcher as well as their place in the scholarly conversation. How might they be taking current work forward? What are they doing that stands out from the work that precedes them? What is their position in the space?

This kind of identity work – which we call OARS, occupying and owning the research space – is critical to constructing a confident and authoritative introduction. As we have seen in Chapter 4, early career writers are reluctant and often nervous to assert themselves in the space. This can show itself by the shortness of their introductions and/or by the disconnection between what they are researching and the literatures of the field.

We now look at the writing of three researchers to show how the move from less to more authoritative scholar shows itself textually in the introduction. The first example comes from Calvin, a writer one year post-PhD, still caught up in his doctoral student identity struggle; the second from Charlotte, a more experienced early career researcher, painfully reticent about her place in the scholarly conversation; the third from two more experienced researchers – Pat and Barbara – asserting themselves, as usual.

Calvin

It is difficult to get the tone and stance right when using literatures in the introduction. What expert readers do *not* want is an extensive recount of all the research related to the writer's topic. But this is what inexperienced writers like Calvin often produce: overlong displays of current research with little evaluation and no argument. We have called this tendency 'he said she said' (Kamler and Thomson, 2006; Thomson and Kamler, 2010), where the writer piles up study after study and lets the experts do the talking, rather than selectively controlling discussions of scholarship and ideas to make their case.

We see this in Calvin's writing (Figure 5.2) based on his recently completed dissertation. This excerpt comes from the introduction to an article for a literacy journal where he tries to situate his research on digital literacies with his year 7/8 students.

> Changing social conditions brought about by globalization and shifts in communication technologies have elicited new, inventive pedagogical responses. They include multiliteracies (NLG, 1996; Cope and Kalantzis, 2000; Albright *et al.*, 2006a; Walsh, 2006), multimodality (Jewit, 2008; Kress *et al.*, 2001; Kress and van Leeuwen, 2001) and design (NLG, 1996; Kress, 2000; 2003; Janks, 2000). These pedagogies build on a range of traditions from critical literacy studies (Lankshear and McLaren, 1993; Lankshear, 1998; A. Luke, 1996; C. Luke, 1992). The New London Group (1996) introduced the term multiliteracies and called for a literacy pedagogy that moved beyond the constraints of linguistic texts to provide students with improved social futures.
>
> Multimodality, like multiliteracies, has also emerged in response to the changing social and semiotic landscape (Jewit, 2008). In terms of literacy education, multimodality is about making meaning through a variety of modes (linguistic, image, audio, gestural, gaze and spatial), where no one mode is necessarily privileged. The theory of multimodality (Kress and van Leeuwen, 2001) focuses on all modes of communication and what it is possible to express and represent in particular contexts. Teachers who enact multiliteracies pedagogies apply the theory of multimodality to explicitly instruct students to analyse all modes in any text (linguistic, audio, visual and so on) or communicative event (talk, gesture, movement and gaze) . . .

Figure 5.2 Excerpt from Calvin's journal article

In a recent analysis of early career literature troubles (Thomson and Kamler, 2010) we examined Calvin's introduction as a site of intense identity work and struggle. The excerpt above is typical of the six pages where Calvin recounts the literatures of his field in excessive detail. What he does is *all* Move 1. He describes the territory ad nauseam. He does not take up a position, detail recent debates or signal where his work might fit in – Move 2 work. We see this textual incapacity to forge a relationship with previous research – to literally insert himself on the page amongst expert scholars – as an identity struggle. One year after candidature, Calvin continues to write as if he is still a doctoral researcher parading his knowledge for examiners. In our experience, this is not an uncommon problem. One of Calvin's reviewers succinctly captured the difficulty for readers of the journal:

> The author tries to use the literature to frame the case study but I don't think it adds very much to the empirical data and the theoretical ground it covers will be well trodden for the readers of this Journal. The writing suggests the author is much more at home with the study than the literature review aspect of the paper and I would suggest that much of this first section be deleted and/or substantially condensed.

Well trodden indeed! Important for the thesis, but not for the journal article that comes from it. Reviewers and readers are not examiners and their purpose for reading is not to credential the writer. Primarily they read to be informed – wowed, even. They know the field, they assume the writer is an expert and they want to see what the article argues or asserts. They want the new and distinctive to be drawn out and made prominent. Clearly, the introduction plays a critical role in this text work, but it requires the writer to find ways to identify and occupy the research space.

Charlotte

Charlotte, an early career researcher in early childhood education, was writing an article for a special issue of a journal. The brief was to use a recent research project to illustrate her approach to visual methodologies and explore its innovation. Unlike Calvin, Charlotte was overly succinct in her introduction, which consisted of only one paragraph (Figure 5.3).

While succinct and to the point, there is not much identity work going on here and no literature work. An aim and argument are articulated. A gap in the literature is asserted, but in such a compressed way it is not exactly clear what the niche is. Is it that not much visual methodology has been used with critical historical theorising, *or* with intergenerational family research, *or* when family

The aims of this article are two-fold. First, it sets out to critically discuss the use of visual methodologies within a cultural-historical theoretical framework in intergenerational research. Second, it argues that family members participating as co-researchers in the generation and analysis of visual data bring new and rich insights to the research process that are not possible when using more traditional methodologies. Despite the popularity of family photography and home video production, there is still little published research framed within cultural-historical theory where visual methodologies have been used with intergenerational families, particularly in relation to family members as co-researchers involved in the generation, selection and analysis of the visual data. This article is written towards addressing this gap in the literature. Examples and illustrations are provided from the researcher's recent work exploring the everyday family practices of three intergenerational Australian families.

Figure 5.3 Charlotte's brief introduction

members are co-researchers? Or all of these things? And if this is a gap, what is this researcher Charlotte doing about it, other than providing examples from her research?

Clearly, one paragraph is too short a space to be doing so much complex locational and identity work. It doesn't yet establish either the territory or the niche so we don't know why she is aiming to do what she wants to do. In the subsequent section of the paper, Charlotte introduces literature on intergenerational family research. This is the place where she is in conversation with her discourse community. But it may not be surprising that, like Calvin, she surveys what others have done, rather than inserting her own work and its contribution to the conversation.

We have found that this overly short introduction with a separate discussion of the literature is not uncommon. Like Charlotte, others struggle to forge a relationship between themselves and more expert researchers. Charlotte's draft was read and discussed in a writing group where it was suggested that she combine the brief one paragraph with some of her literature work but *try* to insert herself into the text so that she occupies some of the research space.

We show a revised introduction in Figure 5.4. This is not yet complete and should be read as in formation. It's work in progress. We present the new bits in capitals to highlight Charlotte's early and sometimes awkward attempt to enter the research space.

The use of the literature enables Charlotte to achieve Move 1 of CARS: establishing a territory and Move 2: establishing a niche for the paper. With guidance from the writing group she was encouraged to insert her stance, her new use of visual methodologies, in the field of intergenerational research.

The aims of this chapter are two-fold. First, the chapter sets out to critically discuss the use of visual methodologies within a cultural-historical theoretical framework in intergenerational research. Second, it argues that family members participating as co-researchers in the generation and analysis of visual data bring new and rich insights to the research process that are not possible when using more traditional methodologies. Despite the popularity of family photography and home video production, there is still little published research framed within cultural-historical theory where visual methodologies have been used with intergenerational families. THE STUDY REPORTED IN THIS ARTICLE IS UNIQUE IN POSITIONING family members as co-researchers involved in the generation, selection and analysis of the visual data. Examples are provided from the researcher's recent work TO ILLUSTRATE A NEW METHODOLOGY FOR exploring the everyday family practices of three intergenerational Australian families.

Over the past 50 years a wealth of data have been generated about families and family relationships (Bengtson et al., 2005). Although the term 'intergeneration' has been used to indicate the generational scope of particular research studies (see for example Bengtson and Roberts, 1991; Chun and Lee, 2006; Dingus, 2008; Harrel-Smith, 2006; Maré and Stillman, 2010; Newman, 2008; Yi et al., 2004) this term can be misleading. The majority of intergenerational studies span only two generations with data being generated from both generations simultaneously; for example grandparents and their grandchildren (Chun and Lee, 2006, Harrel-Smith, 2006, Wise, 2010); parents and their adolescent children (Yi et al., 2004) or older parents and their middle aged children as in the seminal work of Bengston and Roberts (1991). Some studies generate data from participants of one generation who comment on their perceptions of other generations; or the data may cover three generations (grandparents, parents and children) but is generated by only the parent generation (for example Boye-Beaman, 1994). The reliance on parental data has been critiqued by Yi, Chang and Chang (2004) suggesting that the findings from such studies are limited.

THIS STUDY IS UNUSUAL IN ACCESSING FOUR GENERATIONS SIMULTANEOUSLY. IT STANDS OUT AS ONE OF A FEW INTERGENERATIONAL STUDIES WHICH GENERATE DATA THROUGH THE USE OF VISUAL METHODOLOGIES, RATHER THAN THE MORE COMMON USE OF SURVEYS AND INTERVIEWS. LIKE THE MORE RECENT RESEARCH by Hedegaard and Fleer, (2008) AND Gillen and Cameron, (2010) it provides methodological and theoretical perspectives on the use of visual methodologies in family research. HOWEVER, IT TAKES THE ADDITIONAL STEP of examining intergenerational relationships and engaging family members as co-researchers involved in decisions concerning data generation, selection and analysis.

Figure 5.4 Charlotte's revised introduction

However, there is still work to do. Charlotte still needs to pay attention to the locational work of Move 1 because we still do not really know why visual research with grandparents is important and what it might contribute to knowledge. It is, however, a giant step forward from the one paragraph introduction. Charlotte is now in the text.

The difficulties faced by Calvin and Charlotte are not unusual. In our workshops we often see the same problems emerging in Tiny Texts. A lack of locational work, an assumption that the place and significance of the work does not have to be argued and a tremendous diffidence about the contribution to be made.

Pat and Barbara

Our third example, shown in Figure 5.5, comes from our own work on doctoral writing. We include it here as an example of a more assertive introduction by writers located firmly in a field. It uses the CARS heuristic in a very straightforward way. It does a version of locational work by calling on relevant literatures in the field and the journal. The literatures are used early on in order to create a mandate for the work, and to elaborate the contribution. The introduction attempts to hook the reader, convincing them that they want to read the whole thing. This is why the introduction also includes an outline of what is to come (not evident in Calvin or Charlotte's writing).

We want to make two important points related to this introduction. Both are layer 3 considerations.

The first point relates to the particular disciplinary and national characteristics of this introduction. It is written in a social science genre in an English language journal. The best way to think about writing to this very broad discourse community is through the analogy of a debating team. The first speaker in a debating team always outlines the case to be made, and then details the contribution each speaker will make to the argument that is being built up. The audience to the debate, the adjudicators and the opposing team know at the beginning of the event the broad shape of things to come. There is no mystery, no surprise.

The same process occurs when an article is introduced in the way we have shown in Figure 5.5. The English language social science article introduction works by outlining the case to be made and how it will be presented through the major sections of the article. The reader knows exactly what is to come. While the details are not revealed, a kind of road map is provided for the reader. Note the syntactic moves here – *we examine, we question, we point to, we see our analysis as.* This approach to writing is often called *deductive*, that is, it provides an explicit line of argument at the outset.

Doctoral researchers can now call on a range of books that offer advice on each and every stage of their research – 'from the moment you type your first word to when you walk into the viva voce examination to defend the completed work' (Oliver, 2004: 3). The proliferation of such books not only reflects the astute marketing strategies of publishers that have been quick to see profit in 'do-it-yourself' (DIY) supervision materials, but also taps into the real anxieties of doctoral students.

    There is no doubt that doctoral research is a complex and challenging undertaking and that students do need support and guidance throughout the process. It is also true that input from doctoral advisors and committees can be usefully supplemented through formal courses; informal peer practices; and well-written, well-theorized books.

Move 1: establishing the territory – the plethora of advice available for doctoral researchers

Our concern, however, is about some of the advice that is on offer, and the possible negative effects it may have on students and on the broader scholarly enterprise.

    As part of ongoing work on doctoral education (Kamler and Thomson, 2004, 2006, 2007), we surveyed advice books. We initially looked at what was available for purchase from one on-line bookseller. Most titles were directly addressed to students. We then went to a university library and found ten shelves devoted to aspects of university teaching and learning, the vast majority of which were in the form of DIY guides and advice books, again for students. Although reading these apparently helpful volumes has not been a uniformly rewarding experience, we were struck by a number of common patterns that emerged across texts.

Move 2: establishing the niche – in this case, a concern about the advice books and their patterning, and an assertion that this needs analysis

In this article we examine the doctoral dissertation advice books as a genre with patterned characteristics and recognizable textual features. We argue that, regardless of the utility of the advice given, the discourse of the novice and the expert through which these texts are written works to position the doctoral researcher as a diminished scholar and to constitute a transmission pedagogy that normalizes the power-saturated relations of protégé and master. The texts also offer a rigid model of the dissertation that follows a set format and style. We question the pedagogical and political implications of such advice and point to alternate

Move 3: occupying and owning the niche – here we offer hints about the analysis to follow and we state the contribution that this analysis will make.

texts that make important moves away from the pervasive advice genre. We see our analysis as part of an ongoing conversation about doctoral writing that moves beyond a focus on tools and techniques to the discursive practices of becoming a scholar (cf; Klingner et al., 2005; Rose and McClafferty, 2001).

(Kamler and Thomson, 2008)

Figure 5.5 CARS Analysis of Kamler and Thomson (2008)

Many other disciplines also follow this initial outlining convention. However, some do not, particularly in the arts and humanities. It is important, as we have proposed in Chapters 2 and 3, that writers check out the genre conventions of the journal to which they propose to contribute, prior to writing. However, we suggest that even if this social science introduction is used in a journal that does not normally follow this convention, it is unlikely that it will lead to rejection. It is familiar territory to most readers of journals.

But other cultural traditions of scholarly writing, for example the French and the Germanic, are not always as explicit as the English language scholarly community about the argument and its presentation through the text. They often use an inductive mode where the reader finds out the argument as they go along.

We have found in writing workshops that scholars educated in other cultural conventions struggle to adapt to the English tradition of self-conscious explication of intentions and argument, often wondering aloud why it is necessary. At the time, we generally suggest that this kind of signposting helps the reader, but we also make clear that this response comes from our position as 'insiders', that is, this level of procedural visibility is something to which we have been accustomed over a long period of time, as have the readers of journals. It is important to note that we are not arguing in workshops – or here – that this is the right or the only way to write an introduction, but rather that it is what generally expected by the English language scholarly community.

We conclude this chapter with a final strategy that brings together CARS and OARS by paying attention to how expert writers in a field introduce their work.

Sentence skeletons

To help writers achieve a more authoritative stance in their introductions we use a strategy which we called *syntactic borrowing* in our previous book (Kamler and Thomson, 2006). Here we re-introduce it because of its power to model new ways of writing, but we rename the strategy sentence skeleton, based on Swales and Feak's (1994) work.

The idea is to select a passage of good writing from the introduction of a published journal article and delete the content. What remains is the skeleton of rhetorical moves made by the author of the article. The skeleton creates a linguistic frame that other writers can emulate and play with.

To illustrate, Figure 5.6 represents the skeleton exhumed from an introduction written by Lavie (2006) for the *Education Administration Quarterly*.

What this skeleton makes explicit, linguistically, is how the writer builds connection with the field and structures his article. In workshops we ask writers to insert the details of their own research into skeletons we provide. We see this as linguistic identity work, a way of early scholars writing themselves into an authoritative stance they may not be able to take alone. Removing the content makes syntax visible; it is not plagiarism. It makes explicit the ways of arguing and locating used in particular discourse communities.

In this article, I discuss the main arguments that deal with the issue of
_____.

In distinguishing between _____ it is my purpose to highlight
_____ by pointing to _____
_____. Besides providing a map of the _____
_____, I assess the extent to which these _____
lay a groundwork for _____. The
article is structured as follows. After giving an overview of the scope of the
_____, I review the particular
_____.

Next, I provide a summary of _____.

Finally, in the last two sections, I consider several implications derived from
_____
_____ and argue that _____.

Figure 5.6 Sentence skeleton (Lavie, 2006)

The writing of Rajee, a PhD student in aeronautical engineering, demonstrates the potential impact of this exercise. Rajee had previously submitted a paper to an international conference documenting a new application of software she had developed to optimise lighter production of aircraft wing structure. While her reviewers gave her minimal, unhelpful commentary (for a more detailed discussion of this review process see Kamler, 2010), she was invited to revise and resubmit. To help Rajee develop a clearer sense of the significance of her project, she used the sentence skeleton from Lavie (2006) set out in Figure 5.6, which she found extremely useful, although it came from a discipline far outside her field. The bold text in Figure 5.7 designates the language of Lavie's (2006) sentence skeleton; the italics are Rajee's language.

In this article, I discuss the main arguments that deal with *the optimisation of Finite Element Models (FEM).* **In distinguishing between** *optimised and non-optimised structures,* **it is my purpose to highlight the** *advantages of an optimised structure* **by pointing to** *weight and cost reductions.* **Besides providing a map of the** *methodologies used,* **I assess the extent to which these** *techniques lay groundwork to improve the structure.* **The article is structured as follows. After giving an overview of the scope of** *shape optimization,* **I review** *the mathematical background of the optimization process.* **Next I provide a summary of** *the ReSHAPE software, including the processes that can be employed in the optimization process.* **Finally, in the last two sections,** *I consider the approach to analysis and results derived from the FEM which is optimised with ReSHAPE* **and argue that** *the optimised structure is lighter and more efficient than the non-optimised structure.*

Figure 5.7 Rajee works with Lavie's sentence skeleton

Lavie's syntax helped Rajee find more authoritative language for situating her own research. She, in effect, stood in the shoes of a more expert writer and adopted their discursive stance. Rajee did not simply insert this exercise into her revised article, but it did help her learn how to argue for the distinctiveness of her contribution. It allowed her to make this more confident assertion in her final draft: 'Shape optimization enables weight savings as well as long term cost benefits, while ensuring the component is structurally sound and can be commercially manufactured'. It also accomplished significant identity work in positioning her as a more assured scholar in her field of aeronautical engineering.

So what, now what?

We've argued that Tiny Texts can be helpful for planning purposes, but the writer still needs more strategies up their proverbial sleeve in order to do the crucial beginning work on the paper proper. We offered three strategies for beginning the journal article: CARS, Create a Research Space; OARS, Occupy a Research Space; and finally Sentence Skeletons, Modelling on Expert Writers. Of course these are not magic bullets. While these strategies *will not* produce a complete introduction, they *will* provide support for both understanding and doing the work of beginning the journal article.

Writing the journal article is, however, an ongoing set of demands – or are these perhaps traps? Even with a road map it's still possible to get bamboozled. That's why, in the next chapter, we concentrate on strategies for middle and end work. For us, this means the work that needs to be done after there is a pretty rough first draft. We reckon that the road map is sufficient to allow writers to produce a complete text, but it will be a text that needs further attention.

Chapter 6

Refining the argument

Having written an abstract, planned and written a first draft, writers know that the article is still not finished. Rarely does an article simply need to be tidied and proofread. The usual way to think about the next stage of writing is to focus on 'revising' and 'editing'. Revising usually signifies larger and more substantive changes to the text, while editing refers to the smaller detail of grammar, spelling, proofreading and general tidying.

In our experience early career writers are often very attached to what they write and are afraid that if they change too much, they will be left with nothing. Editing is more often attended to because this seems less drastic and more tangible. Unfortunately, much writing advice on offer reinforces this kind of editing at the expense of revising.

We don't use this revise and edit framework. This accords with research conducted by Mike Rose (2009), a professor at UCLA and an academic writing specialist, who examined the reasons why many people find writing so difficult. His research showed the dangers of premature- and over-editing, and the importance of alternative strategies. According to Rose, if a writer starts to edit a text without having a useful set of syntactic strategies – such as using headings and subheadings or manoeuvring topic sentences for paragraphs – they cannot bring a logical order to what is written. They lack the meso-level strategies necessary for getting focus. Over-editing, attending to the fine details, can compound problems as writers are stuck in between macro-mess and the micro-textual manipulations. They need a way of tackling the overall text and its argument. Rose concludes that if a text is disorganised, then it needs to be restructured before it can be finely edited.

We have called this chapter 'Refining the argument' because we are interested in the 'organisation' work to which Rose refers. This meso-level work on the text is often glossed over or packaged in ways that are vague, to say the least.

For example, we have recently come across a set of writing advice tips that lists ten steps for revising a chapter or article. We have not formally cited this source in part because we do not want to name and shame the author, but also because this advice is pretty typical of what is out there in print and online. The first three steps are: remove all unnecessary information, reorganise, and check for missing information. At no stage are readers given any assistance to think about the actual criteria which might be used to guide decisions about what information should be removed, reorganised, or inserted. The remaining seven steps simply consist of more exhortations to revise, revise, revise and then edit.

Refining the argument, as opposed to revising and editing, means honing, crafting and moulding the text until it has the characteristics of a good journal article, namely:

- a tight focus which allows one or, at most, two ideas to be dealt with, and about three or four major points to be made;
- a synthesis of research literatures which refers *only* to the key texts and debates on which the article builds and to which it makes a contribution;
- theory, if it is used, explained largely in the writer's own words and as economically as possible, referring only to the particular theoretical aspects that are needed in the paper;
- citations which do not crowd out the text; the majority of the word allowance should be devoted to the paper itself, which is, after all, the contribution.

In this chapter we focus, in particular, on the argument and the moves that have and have not been made. We see this as middle work and end work. Once the beginning of the text has clearly established the territory in which the research is located, designated the niche and owned and occupied it (as shown in Chapter 5), the writer's task is to see how well the text accomplishes the introductory aspiration. It is also critical to ascertain whether, at the end of the article, the case is not simply summarised, but asserted and its implications made explicit.

We have developed four refining strategies: mapping the ground; naming the moves; developing a meta-commentary; and crunching the conclusion. These all rely on a geographic metaphor, which assists writers to gain a helicopter view of their text. The helicopter allows the writer to rise above the text, see it as a whole and view its features from a distance. The detail is stripped out. Writers can hover over one place as long as is necessary to attend to the bigger textual landscape. They can also hone in on smaller and specific features. They can then move across the topography in order to see the connections and pathways that are provided for readers – or not.

We begin with the most distanced viewing of the text, the highest altitude from which we can view our writing.

Mapping the ground

First draft in hand, the writer's challenge is to read the textual landscape of their draft article as if this were an exercise in grounded theory. Grounded theory works not from an imposed frame, but from the data itself: the task is to find the patterns, or themes, in the detail. The researcher reads their data to find ways of grouping it together and then gives each of these data clumps a label. We are suggesting that writers can take the same kind of approach to their article. Here, the data that writers are working with is a first draft which has the substance of the argument and its supporting evidence.

The 'mapping the ground' strategy is the equivalent to surveying from the vantage point of the helicopter. The writer must rise far enough above the text to see its dominant features. The purpose is to reveal the structure of the text, and any structural problems. We have developed this strategy from the 'reverse outline' which we first saw in the blog 'explorations of style' (www.explorations ofstyle.wordpress.com).

In our experience, there are two dominant types of textual landscape produced by early career writers: one with too few sections identified and one with too many. We offer a different mapping approach for each.

1. Mapping the featureless landscape

The featureless landscape is characterised by having large sections of writing and almost no headings. Readers and reviewers often get frustrated when faced with a long middle section that seems to include a number of topics and ideas that could usefully be separated out in order to make the argument clearer. How long is this going on? Where is it going? What is the writer saying that is most important?

The goal is to first of all identify the 'moves', the major chunks of argument that have not been marked. Each chunk should be given a sentence. These sentences should be listed separately as an outline to see if they follow logically.

Some reorganisation may also be required. Major omissions can be identified, as can superfluous and repetitive writing. The relative weighting of each section (this is where we count words) can also be assessed. The refined outline can then be used to produce subheadings.

So, the questions to ask of the featureless textual landscape are:

- What are the major chunks of writing about?
- How can they best be labelled?
- Are these chunks in the right order?
- What can be removed?

- What needs to be added?
- How much space is devoted to each chunk?
- And, what is the flow within each chunk? (We do more on this soon.)

2. Mapping the busy landscape

The busy landscape is characterised by many, many sections, none of which are necessarily connected. These sections are typically short and there is generally a gross imbalance between them. Readers and reviewers get frustrated when faced with numerous sections, none of which seem connected to each other. What do each of these pieces add up to? Which of these is more important than the others? What's the point?

The writer needs to identify which of these sections, if any, are needed, which might be amalgamated, which might be rebalanced, and which might be renamed or omitted. Again, the strategy is to list each section in order as an outline sentence. The relative weighting of each section can be assessed by doing a word and/or page count. Major omissions can be identified as can superfluities and repetitions.

The questions to ask of a busy textual landscape are:

- How many chunks are there?
- What are these called?
- Are they in a logical order?
- How much space is devoted to each?
- How might they be combined and reordered?
- What needs to be removed?
- What is the flow within each chunk?

Both of these strategies allow the writer to see whether the overall argument is as intended, and has the required sequence in order to make sense.

It may be that the first draft has used the default IMRAD structure – Introduction, Methods, Report and Discuss. In our experience IMRAD lends itself to a report format, and not an argument. This in turn often leads to a telegraphed introduction (see Chapter 5 on what beginning work entails). Most importantly, the terms Report and Discussion do not foreground argument. The only place argument *can* go is in the discussion and this often leads writers to produce either a featureless (no subheadings) or busy (too many headings) discussion landscape. Very few journals actually require the IMRAD structure even though analyses of articles may show that it is the dominant practice. Writers who have used it might use the mapping strategy to restructure the draft, so that the next refined iteration becomes an argument. This may be uncomfortable work, because in mapping there is no place to hide!

Once the structure is sorted out, and the right chunks are in the desired order, there is the question of what to call them.

Naming the moves

Articles need to use headings and subheadings. These help the reader understand the sequence of steps in the argument, and the major themes that hold sets of details together. Sensible advice can be found on the use of headings in Chapter 4 of Patrick Dunleavy's (2003) book on authoring a thesis; in Nygaard's (2008) chapter evocatively entitled *Breaking up the gray mass.* We too discuss the importance of headings in our book on doctoral writing (Kamler and Thomson, 2006: 96–99). But here we want to think about headings and subheadings in relation to the meaning work that they accomplish in the journal article.

Headings are an important tool in the journal article toolkit. Because the journal article is always word-limited, we need to make use of every linguistic opportunity to present the argument to the reader. And because many readers are busy academics, they may, in fact, just be scanning the abstract and sub-headings to see if the article is worth reading more fully.

When we run workshops we often have people do precisely this – scan-read an article by looking at the abstract, the introduction, the headings and subheadings and the conclusion. If these key pieces of the article are working, then it is surprising how much a reader can gain through this quick exercise. When the readers can't make sense of the article, it is almost always because one or more of these key textual features are missing or are badly named.

Articles which use a version of the IMRAD default structure as the major section headings are much harder to scan than those which provide more information. It's a bit like coming to the canned food section of the supermarket to find tins which are simply marked 'soup'. What kind of soup is it, one might wonder. Thick? Thin? Vegetable? Meat? If the can is more specifically labelled then it is easier to anticipate what is inside. Similarly, a 'findings' section which uses a colon, as in *Findings: plus a phrase about the major content,* or an alternative heading to denote what is 'inside' the section, is much more illuminating to the reader.

Subheadings do not simply tell the reader what is coming up – they show the kind of thinking process that has gone on to make sense of the material. They offer categories, terminology and conceptual frames – in other words, the scholarly work that has been undertaken.

The following example is drawn from a theoretical paper, sometimes called a think piece. These types of articles usually read across a body of literature and, in this case, contemporary policy, in order to offer an argument about how policy and practice might be different. They not only require good knowledge of the discourse community, in this case within the discipline of geography, but also a substantive quantum of reading in the relevant areas. The writer speaks with considerable authority as an expert with credibility in the field. This is not a given, and no matter what the writer's reputation is, every article must be constructed skilfully anew.

First we present the title and the abstract (Abstract 6.1) by Linda McDowell (2004), an eminent British geographer. We have divided the abstract into our four moves to show how they appear in this particular text. Then in Table 6.1 we analyse the headings that are used in the article to show how the argument is being built up through the beginning, middle and end work.

Work, workfare, work/life balance and an ethic of care

LOCATE: In this paper, I build on Paul Cloke's (2002) provocative argument about the necessity of developing an ethical stance in human geography.

FOCUS: I do this, however, through an assessment of the implications of a number of changes – in the nature of the labour market in Great Britain, in the assumptions that lie behind welfare provision under New Labour and in the position of women and men in Britain – rather than through an emphasis on the Christian values that infused Cloke's argument.

REPORT: I show how the dominance of an individualistic ethos pervades both the labour market and the welfare state, undermining notions of collective welfare and an ethic of care, within the wider context of the hegemony of a neoliberal ideology in global as well as national politics.

ARGUE: If an ethic of care is to be (re)instituted, it will demand wide-reaching changes in the ways in which organizations and institutions operate at a range of spatial scales as well as new sets of responsibilities towards co-workers, members of households and the wider public. I conclude by considering some of the implications of such an ethic for everyday practices within the academy.

(McDowell, 2004)

Abstract 6.1 McDowell abstract, 2004

There is a clear relationship between the organisation of this abstract and the article itself. As Table 6.1 shows, the writer designs the headings to signal the moves of the argument. Just reading the headings already provides some indication of the subject matter and, taken together with the abstract, leaves the reader with a very clear notion of why the paper has been written, the problem it addresses, and the conclusion that is reached. This would not be possible with generic titling.

We can see from this example that, in middle work, headings and sub-headings need to be thought of as part of the process of signalling the higher order analytic work that provides the material from which the argument is crafted.

Faltering middle work gives reviewers cause for concern. Reassurances can be given in the detail of methods sections about the rigour of the approach taken, but this then needs to be demonstrated through the assured use of textual tools throughout the article. Thinking seriously about headings and subheadings is a sure way to signal to the reader what is coming – and what has been done to produce a particular line of argument.

This is not easy and early career researchers often need someone to help.

Table 6.1 Headings that convey argument

Headings		The moves
I.	Introduction: the dominance of neoliberalism	The territory of the article (neoliberalism) is established
II.	Competitiveness, individualisation and gender divisions of labour	Problems within the territory (neoliberalism) are discussed
III.	New divisions of labour and patterns of working life	Key areas where these problems manifest are delineated and, we can assume, evidence is provided
IV.	Workfare policies	
V.	Discourses of parenting	
VI.	An ethic of care rather than an ideal of independence: towards social solidarity	An alternative approach is suggested
VII.	British universities	Implications are drawn out, in this case for British universities. Questions are raised about the future
VIII.	What are universities for?	

Learning to refine headings and subheadings

Veronica and Nola are early career researchers who are writing their first journal article from their PhDs. Veronica had finished her research but is still in the process of writing the thesis. Nola had just completed the PhD and was beginning to publish from the thesis. Pat and Barbara acted as their publication brokers (see Chapter 7 for a detailed discussion of publication brokers) helping them refine their respective arguments through mapping moves and revising subheadings.

Veronica's research was an ethnographic study of the implementation of English healthy schools policy, and she was trying to write the middle data chapters. She found it very difficult to sort out which findings and analysis should go where. Pat suggested co-writing an article as a potential means of sorting out what the problem was.

After jointly producing an abstract, Veronica sent Pat a first draft with the following email:

> I am really struggling with the linkages (no flow) and I may be guilty of getting some of the different arguments mixed up in it. I spent a long time waffling about nominalisation before realising that's not what I'm supposed to be doing.

When Pat opened the draft she saw ten pages of text with no headings at all. It was a featureless landscape. She decided that what she needed to do was to map the territory, that is read for the major chunks, and then provide some headings that would help Veronica to not only see what text went where, and to divide it up, but to help carry the argument along.

The headings and subheadings that Pat provided were these:

1. Introduction: Healthy schools policy
2. The ethnographic research into healthy schools
3. The organisation of healthy schools policy at Lowbridge
4. Performing health (later changed to The performatisation of policy at Lowbridge)
   - External framing and pressures
   - Internal standardisation
   - Internal monitoring (self-regulation)
5. The consequences of this approach (later changed to Performativity and health)
   - Instrumentalisation of relationships
   - Culture of fear for staff
   - Staff needs at odds with professional duties

- Divisions created between staff
- Student cynicism about purposes and practices

6. Conclusion: The paradox of performing health (later changed to Ethnography and performing health)

Veronica was relieved to see these headings and her immediate email back to Pat said, 'Thanks. Very helpful as I was getting lost in it. Changes look really good'. Eventually, in response to reviewer comments which asked that both performativity and ethnography be highlighted more strongly, three further refining changes were made to the headings (shown in brackets above).

It was no accident that after working on this article Veronica made considerable headway on the thesis, using the same two strategies of mapping and headings to sort out the content and flow of her data chapters.

Working with headings was also useful to Nola, whose early draft could be described as a busy landscape (rather than a featureless one, like Veronica's). Nola's research was a four-year ethnographic study of the scholastic/life strategies used by six African American adolescent males in an urban US high school. Her focus on three pairs of best friends who comprised a friendship network provided a wealth of data on how these young men negotiated success and failure across a variety of contexts (out-of-school, in-school, at home and with peers).

When she brought her draft to a writing group Barbara facilitated, she was struggling to narrow her focus. Which boys should she look at? All or some? And how could she best convey their strategies for making it at school in the limited word length available? In a section called 'Findings' she presented her data on the boys using the following eight subheadings:

1. From schoolboy to coolboy: Codeswitching identity for success (1 page)
2. The coolboys: Success with peers (2 pages)
3. The schoolboys: Success in school (2 pages)
4. Misunderstood: Struggles for identity reconstruction and classroom success (.5 page)
5. The problem of Kobe and Norbit (2 pages)
6. The bullet resounds: Violence and academic trajectory (1.5 pages)
7. Parenthood as pivot: Self-created opportunities for identity reconstruction (5 pages)
8. Petey P: Seizing the opportunity (4 pages)

The headings give some indication of Nola's struggle. Eight headings are a lot and the sections are very uneven in their balance and distribution across the paper, with some as short as half a page, and others up to five pages long. Two of the headings name the boys (*Kobe and Norbit; Petey P.*), the others do not. And when these sections were closely analysed with Barbara, it became clear there was an enormous amount of detail and a constant moving back and forth between the boys' stories, with few of the sections focusing on particular boys. While this made sense to Nola, it was confusing to an outside reader who had not spent four years researching with these young men. Nola's original title 'Misunderstood: Strategies for cross-contextual success among African American adolescent males in urban environments' also gestured to the topic of her thesis, rather than focusing her argument for this particular journal article.

In three subsequent drafts and meetings with Barbara, Nola worked to refine her focus to issues of identity reconstruction. She rewrote the abstract several times and rewrote the title to the more specific and argumentative: 'Identity reconstruction as strategy for academic success: Second chances for African American Adolescent males'. Nola was deeply committed to countering deficit-based perspectives on African American adolescent males and this revision better captures her intent. So do the revised subheadings in her penultimate draft:

1. Kanye: Codeswitching identity to achieve success across contexts (5 pages)
2. Kobe and Norbit: Using parenthood as self-created opportunity for identity reconstruction (5 pages)
3. Petey P: Seizing tragedy as a second chance for school success (4.5 pages)

Eight headings have been reduced to three. Each section is now of similar length and better organised to focus on particular boys (the boys are named before the colon). The headings are also used to name a key identity reconstruction strategy used by the boys to succeed at school. This makes the organisation of the data clearer and the moves of her argument more visible to a reader. It paves the way later on in the article for Nola to critique a schooling system that leaves the major responsibility for success to chance or the ingenuity of students without an equal commitment by schools themselves.

Developing a meta-commentary

As well as getting the moves right and refining the headings and subheadings, additional work is required to carry the argument through the text, to construct its flow. It is helpful to think of an article as having two narratives. One is the substantive commentary of the article. The other, as Graf and Birkenstein (2010) put it, is a meta-text, the equivalent of a Greek chorus which stands to the side to explain the meaning of the text to its audience. Graf and Birkenstein talk about two texts joined at the hip, one of which makes the argument. The other distinguishes 'your views from others they may be confused with, anticipating and answering objections, connecting one point to another, explaining why your claim might be controversial and so forth' (130).

We prefer the notion of meta-commentary to the more commonly used notion of making effective transitions. Providing transitions tends to focus on technical connections between paragraphs and sections. Writers might be offered advice such as: 'avoid unnecessary transition words, e.g. furthermore, moreover, in addition'. Writers are pointed to the ends and beginnings of paragraphs and sections, and the words that are used to get from one to another. This is akin, in our view, to jumping between stepping stones rather than constructing the pathway through the article. The focus on fixing transitions tends to the superficial, rather than going to the substantive issues of argumentative flow and the ways in which rhetorical tools can assist the reader to follow the reasoning. It's not that transitions do not need to be attended to, but rather that they need to be thought of more holistically in the context of the argument in its entirety. Hence we use Graf and Birkenstein's notion of a meta-commentary.

There is good reason for seriously engaging with meta-commentary. It is easy for readers to get lost in a complex argument. We have certainly had the experience of writing something and then finding a reader response which seems to misunderstand the point we are trying to make. When we have examined our text we can see that the misreading may well be due to the lack of appropriate meta-commentary. All writers want to avoid provoking reactions they didn't intend, allowing their arguments to be mistaken for ones they didn't want to make; or having readers focus in on details of the argument but miss its overall significance. The writer may have written correctly and elegantly, but as Graf and Birkenstein say

> no matter how straightforward a writer you are, readers still need you to help them grasp what you really mean. Because the written word is prone to so much mischief and can be interpreted in so many different ways, we need metacommentary to keep misinterpretations and other communication misfires at bay.

> (Graf and Birkenstein, 2010: 131)

There are different kinds of meta-commentaries and Graf and Birkenstein offer some very helpful templates (135–136) as a guide to their formulation and use. For example, in order to ward off potential misunderstandings they suggest that writers say something like:

> Essentially I am arguing not that we should give up the policy, but that we should monitor its effects more closely.

This is not to say . . . , but rather . . ..

X is concerned less with . . . than with . . ..

In order to alert readers to an elaboration of a previous idea, which Graf and Birkenstein say is analogous to saying, 'In case you didn't get it the first time, I'll try saying the same thing in a different way', they suggest an appropriate meta-commentary could go something like:

In other words . . .

To put it another way . . .

What X is saying here is that . . .

Even though these examples might seem obvious, we think it can be very helpful to consult these kinds of templates in the process of refining the text.

To illustrate the use of some of the different strategies Graf and Birkenstein identify, we explore two examples. The first provides a road map to a section of a paper. The second combines warding off potential misunderstandings with alerting readers to an elaboration of a previous idea.

The first example comes from a journal article by Pat (Thomson, 2010); a think-piece which challenges the dominant interpretations of both advocacy and critical writings on school self-management (Figure 6.1). This is contentious work and it requires a careful elaboration of how the text will be presented and what it will cover.

Part A: The phenomenon of headteacher desire for autonomy

In this section **I present evidence** that policy shifts to extend school autonomy have been accompanied by expressions of headteacher satisfaction and also the desire for still further extension of apparent freedoms. **I suggest** that these headteacher behaviours are relatively constant over a relatively long period of time, across school sectors and in several different places **(although I mainly discuss** Australia and England). **In making this generalisation, I do not want to suggest that this means** that there are no differences between sectors, systems and times. **Rather I want to argue**, after Bourdieu, that headteachers are disposed, by virtue of the game they are in, to press for more authority and that this has been a relative constant in the field, despite the relative autonomies of time-space. **This** desire, I **suggest in conclusion, is important to understanding** the logic of much of their practice. **I thus present a selection of evidence** spread over time, space and sectors, **to illustrate this point.**

Figure 6.1 Meta-commentary argumentative moves, example 1

We have put in bold the words and phrases that signal the argumentative work Pat is doing. These provide a meta-commentary which outlines the shape of the argument and what it will and won't do.

We can see that Pat works in this section to not only outline the argument she will make, but also to anticipate potential objections and misreadings, in order to justify the approach she will take and the reader can expect. The anticipation of objections is essential in making a persuasive argument and is always accomplished through these types of rhetorical moves.

The second example comes from Lillis and Curry's *Academic writing in the global context: The politics and practices of publishing in English* (2010). The book documents research on the publication experiences of multilingual scholars working in Spain, Portugal, Hungary and the Slovak Republic. In the section we present in Figure 6.2, they are clarifying the benefits of previous work on discourse communities and communities of practice, while arguing for a new synthesis that incorporates an ignored and potentially controversial framework. Thus their meta-commentary is a careful explication of their position.

Discourse community **proves particularly useful for** emphasising the discourses associated with the specific disciplinary group or community, notably the specific texts and genres (e.g. Johns 1997; Swales 1990, 2004), **whereas** *community of practice* **emphasises** the activities or practices associated with particular groups and the ways in which individuals engage in them (Belcher 1994; Wenger 1998). **Research** in academic literacy **draws on both notions to explore** the relationship between texts and practices, that is, the ways in which people learn the rules governing both texts and practices and thus participate in their maintenance and development (Candlin and Hyland 1999; Flowerdew 2000; Myers, 1990; Prior, 1998). **In aiming to characterize** who scholars are writing for, **notions of** discourse community and community of practice **are clearly important, but it is also important not to lose sight of a third notion** of community, that of *speech community* (Hymes 1974), which helps to foreground, in particular, the significance of linguistic medium in academic text production. **Although the notion** of speech community **has limitations** – particularly that it implies a focus only on the spoken word – **it is important for the very reason for which it has often been dismissed** in academic literacy research: **it foregrounds the importance of** the relationship between the individual and his or her local sociolinguistic context. The local sociolinguistic context is **often minimised in discussion of** discourse communities, where 'discourse' is used to emphasise written texts . . . **Here, we simply wish to stress that ignoring the notion** of speech communities in explorations of academic literacy practices **masks a significant aspect of** the interests driving the research and writing activity of scholars who are working in languages in addition to English.

Figure 6.2 Meta-commentary argumentative moves, example 2

We have put in bold the phrases which are used to elaborate their new contribution, to criticise (gently) its absence from prior scholarship and to emphasise the benefits of their approach.

In both examples we can see the meta-commentary at work, carefully directing the reader to the ways in which they should read the text that follows. In each case we see a delineation of what the text is and is not going to do – in other words, there is a direction to the reader not to assume that a particular reading is the case. They are also being shepherded away from being critical of the offering on the basis of misunderstanding the writer's intention. The meta-commentary defines, delimits and directs.

Having attended to the middle of the text, and the work needed to refine and clarify the argument, we now move to the end work of the article, the conclusion.

Crunching the conclusion

The ending, or conclusion, as it is more generally known, has to avoid multiple pitfalls. An ending must pithily summarise the argument and the evidence presented, evoking what has been covered, without repeating everything tediously. A conclusion is not the time to invoke déjà vu! It must also not introduce new information or ideas, something that novice writers find difficult to avoid. At the same time it must elaborate the contribution and delineate its implications, while also modestly but assertively staking a claim. *This is my research. These are my findings. This is my argument. It is a significant contribution to the field. It matters. Here's why and how.* It also must leave an impression – sotto voce – *and don't you forget it, here is what you know that you didn't know before.* This is the crunch.

We introduced the term crunch in Chapter 4 when we discussed the importance of titles capturing the gist of the article. In the conclusion, the crunch is what we want the reader to remember. It is what we hope that they will write in their literature survey, as in: *Smith (2012) suggests that . . .* It is the claim that we make, based firmly in the findings, directed towards a broader problem/debate/niche/conversation within the discourse community. It is our one second of fame, our insertion into the scholarly conversation.

The conclusion must accomplish this work without being trite, over-inflated, banal or hesitant. This is why the conclusion is so difficult to write.

Indeed, we hate endings. We harbour a quiet foreboding about how we will sign off this book. There seems to be no scholarly equivalent to Charlotte Bronte's 'Reader, I married him', aptly described as a 'victorious economy' by

Observer columnist, Kate Kellaway (2011). Oh for a victorious economy for every journal article we write! The reason for our dislike of conclusions is that we often feel as if we've already said it. And it is difficult to sum up another way of saying the same thing in fewer words. With punch. However, a weak conclusion detracts badly from the overall article, because it is, after all, the last thing the reader encounters. It is important, therefore, to think about what it is the reader should remember.

Focusing on a crisp ending sentence is, of course, not what is required. The most important aspect of the conclusion in a journal article is to refer back to the location of the paper and the locational work that was accomplished via the beginning section, the introduction. At the outset, the article was situated in a broader context – a problem in the field, a puzzle in the literatures, a blind spot, something still to be done. The Locate work argued that this was important and the paper would address this. The conclusion must take up this thread and summarise the argument made and its implications in the light of this Locate work.

It is thus sensible to refer back to the abstract and the title of the paper when beginning the actual job of writing the conclusion. It is sometimes helpful to consciously use the appropriate mapping and/or meta-commentary language: *I have argued in this paper firstly, secondly and finally. In conclusion . . ..* It is also helpful to think about the final statement which needs to re-emphasise the contribution and its significance.

We offer one extended example to illustrate how an ending might happen. We have chosen an article from a journal which serves an interdisciplinary discourse community located in the field of childhood studies. The community shares some common assumptions drawn largely from sociological under-standings of the ways in which 'childhood' is a culturally constructed cate-gory, but it also has a shared commitment to seeing children as expert witnesses to their own lives. This leads to a sustained interest in methodological questions about children and their role in research. This article by Chris Pole (2007), an experienced and well-regarded member of the social science community, addresses the question of adult researcher and child relationships.

We begin with the title and abstract (Abstract 6.2) to show the Locate work that the writer does.

We can see already that the abstract locates the paper in the current interest in researching children's everyday lives. It has however collapsed together the Focus and Report and the reader is thus less clear than they might be about the actual empirical study that is used to make the argument. Nevertheless, the article would, we suggest, make a researcher in the area curious because Pole promises to make a case for embodied reflexivity which will show a potential

Researching children and fashion: an embodied ethnography

LOCATE: Child-centred research methods present a range of opportunities for the researcher to gather rich and detailed data on many aspects of the lives of children.

FOCUS and REPORT: This article examines the experience of using such methods in the context of a study of children as consumers of clothing and fashion. Its principal concern is with the application of an embodied reflexivity to the experience of fieldwork with an 8-year-old girl in intimate settings.

ARGUE: The article argues that the current climate of concern about child abuse and paedophilia may be at odds with research approaches that necessitate an intimacy between child and researcher.

(Pole, 2007)

Abstract 6.2 Pole abstract, 2007

conflict between research goals and policy practices about child protection and safe-guarding. The beginning work in the introduction of the article proper further elaborates a key context for the argument, that of ethnographic research, a methodological approach which requires an ongoing trusting relationship between the researcher and the researched.

It is not too hard to imagine, having read the title and the abstract, that despite the lack of focus and report, the writer is going to go on to elaborate the need for ethnographers to establish trusting and intimate relations with subjects, and show how this happens in practice, but then argue that when this actually occurs with children, the ethnographic approach may well fall foul of safeguarding practices.

It is worth noting that the title does not give much hint of the dilemma that is central to the paper: ethnography in a time of moral panic about child protection. Rather, it suggests the reader might read about children's clothing choices. As a meta-commentary this title does not really crunch the significant argument to be made in the article.

We show in Figure 6.3 how the conclusion to Pole's article, as we have suggested conclusions must, returns to this broader dilemma to make his case.

Conclusion text

This article has sought to apply a form of embodied reflexivity to the research process. This has allowed me to analyse aspects of my research practice that may have otherwise been overlooked or taken for granted. An embodied perspective has facilitated a fundamental analysis of the relationship between researcher and research participants, researcher and research setting, and researcher and the substantive focus of the study.

However, for the significance of the body, both as a physical entity and an organizing concept for the research, to be fully realized, it needs to be seen within contemporary concerns about childhood and the perceived risks associated with it.
   Current concerns about stranger danger, child abduction and paedophilia are in many respects concerns about the violation of children's bodies. Moreover, children and childhood may be seen to embody an innocence and purity (Ennew, 1986) that extends beyond the individual child to represent childhood as a whole. Threats or violation of an individual child therefore become symbolic of violation of childhood per se. For example, media portrayals of Sarah Payne, and more recently Holly Wells and Jessica Chapman at the time of their abduction and dreadful murders, have imbued them with an almost mystical quality, as angelic bodies (golden curls, healthy sun tans, smiling faces, gingham check school uniform), pictures of innocence, to which many parents can relate. They have, therefore, come to represent (female) children more generally. Violation of these bodies has become symbolic of a violation of childhood and innocence themselves. As Mason and Falloon (2001) argue, child protection is based on a socialization paradigm in which concern is expressed not merely for the child as he or she exists but also for what he or she might become. It is, then, a concern not just for the future of the individual child but for all our futures.

The application of an embodied perspective to our methodology inevitably brings these issues closer. In particular, as ethnographers, working with, rather than on, children and their lives, we seek a degree of intimacy that is not available to other kinds of researchers. However, in doing so, it is

Textual moves

Summary of what the article set out to do and the benefits of the analysis.

Elaboration of the policy of child protection with strong emphasis on contemporary concerns. This is a claim for the timely significance of the article.

Reiteration of the necessity of an embodied perspective to ethnography. The shift to 'we' encompasses and

imperative that we recognize the need to protect the children with whom we work and respect their right to privacy and anonymity. By the simple fact that we are there and are involved, this intimacy is an embodied intimacy. When those with whom we work, such as children, may be seen as vulnerable, then such intimacy may pose a threat to that vulnerability.	incorporates the reader into the writer's argument.
If this is the case, rather than bringing researcher and child closer together, child-centred methods may actually result in the construction of constraints and boundaries between researcher and child.	Implications spelled out for the field.
For those of us committed to the intimacy afforded by child-focused research methods and their capacity to allow us a glimpse of the interior world of the child, there is a need not only for an embodied reflexivity, but also an embodied transparency in our work. This means that while we will not shirk sensitive subjects or look for corporeal distance behind more remote methods, we will be constantly aware not only of the possibilities offered by child-centred methods, but also of the difficulties they might pose to researchers and to children.	Concluding statement about a potential resolution. The use of 'us' and 'we' again brings the reader into the writer's resolution.

Figure 6.3 Analysis of moves in Pole's (2007) conclusion

Pole has successfully ended the article in a compelling way. We know the key elements of the argument, why they are significant, why they are relevant now, what the problems are and potentially how to resolve them.

This is, of course, not the only way to conclude an article.

We refer the reader to The Academic Phrase Bank at Manchester University (www.phrasebank.manchester.ac.uk) which contains further examples of meta-commentary for concluding. Their templates include: summarising your content; restatement of aims; summarising the findings; suggesting implications; significance of the findings; limitations of the current study; recommendations for further research; and implications/recommendations for practice or policy. Most of these 'starters' are written in a post-positivist paradigm and may be inappropriate for at least some social science writing. However, many can be rephrased so that they fit a more post-critical epistemology, and they will still prove useful.

So what, now what?

Having a full draft requires writers to take a distanced stand on their writing. This is always easier said than done. It is not that we are necessarily attached to our words, although sometimes this is the case. It's often that when we have a first draft done, it feels as if we have finished. That's why the notion of a small amount of revising and editing is so attractive. Instead, we have proposed the notion of refining the text and offered strategies for middle and end work. These allow writers to take a distanced view of their writing and to see it as malleable and amenable to structural adjustments. We hope that readers find these as helpful as we do.

So, after refining, refining and more refining the article is finally complete. It has been read and critiqued and re-read. It is formatted in the appropriate style and anonymised for reviewers. All the references are complete and careful proofreading for spelling, typos and syntax errors is done. It's as ready as it can be. An hour or so on the journal website to submit the article.

Phew, it's in!

Chapter 7

Engaging with reviewers and editors

You may remember the film *The Shining* where Jack Nicholson chops down the door with an axe, grinning madly. The woman behind the door screams in terror as he sticks his head through the door and ominously grimaces, 'Here's Johnny!' This is the moment when the reviewer comments arrive back in the inbox and we are terrified to click to open the email. Finally, the decision on the article is here. Our metaphorical Johnny smirks, 'I'm back'. And we know we have to deal with him.

This chapter addresses the gritty reality of getting the journal article back. If there was labour in constructing the article, there is certainly labour in dealing with its return and the accompanying reviewers' comments. Our goal was to produce and submit a quality article and we got there. But – not really. The horrible realisation that there is still so much to do dawns on us. We're not really there yet. And this realisation is always emotionally draining because we now have to accept the need to unstitch and unpick the careful argument we crafted and thought was complete.

This chapter demystifies the process. We explore the kinds of feedback that writers typically receive from journals and interrogate the views of publishers, reviewers and the reviewed. We canvass the essential role of publication brokers and present strategies for approaching the revise and resubmit process. We illustrate how to decode reviewer reports and write back that important letter to the editor. In order to do this work, we return to the notions of discourse community and the layers 1, 2, and 3 that we introduced and explained in the first three chapters.

We begin by thinking about reviewers as members of the discourse community of the journal to which we submitted our article.

Engaging with the discourse community

Sending an article to a journal to be reviewed is not simply acquiring two or three readers. Referees are trusted members of the discourse community that read and support the journal. They have been selected because they know and can speak for the more general readership: they also have expertise about topics related to the article, may have published in the same area or may even appear in the article's reference list. Some journals, *The British Journal of Sociology of Education* for example, only use their editorial boards as reviewers, making the review process a much more consistent expression of a particular 'take' on a field. Most journals, however, have a database of reviewers to call on. The vast majority of editors now report that it is harder to get people to review and that they often have to cast the net wider than might be desirable or to call on the same people over and over again. It is the wide-net approach that is generally responsible for widely divergent and often conflicting reviews (more on this later).

All journals use reviewer proformas which typically ask for a global recommendation: acceptance, minor revisions, major revisions or rejection. Reviewers are also sometimes offered categories of response about the fit with the journal, the structure of the article, and the quality of the writing. There is always space provided for reviewers to make additional comments to the author and, sometimes, confidential comments to the editor. Editors often provide specific guidance on the tone of these comments, suggesting that reviewers focus on the positive and offer concrete suggestions for changes, rather than vague homilies. Despite this scaffolding, what reviewers actually write in the space for comments varies enormously.

When writers receive comments back from the editor, with reviewer comments attached, they are not simply being told what revisions to make. They are now in an asynchronous conversation with the discourse community. The writer has sent the discourse community something and they have responded. And the editor is a powerful arbiter of this conversation.

Figure 7.1 outlines the way in which reviewer recommendations are actioned.

It is relatively uncommon to receive unconditional acceptance from the reviewing process. Any of the other three options – major and minor revisions and rejection – are the most likely. Minor revisions are, or ought to be, a cause for celebration. We want to examine the last two possible fates of the journal article in more detail: rejection and revise and resubmit, since these are the most difficult to handle.

What happens after the editor has made a decision

Unconditional acceptance
These articles are forwarded to the editor who will then send them to the publisher to be copyedited.

Accept with minor revisions
The editor will forward a copy of the referees' reports to the author with a request that the revisions be made. The author should then return the revised article to the editor; it then goes to the publisher for copyediting.

Revise and resubmit
The editor will forward a copy of the referees' reports to the author inviting them to resubmit the article after it has been revised to take into account the comments made in the referees' evaluation reports. Once resubmitted it will most often be returned to the original referees for their assessment.

Reject
The editor will return the submission and the referees' reports to the author, who will not be invited to resubmit the article.

Figure 7.1 Typical journal decisions and their consequences

Rejection

The word rejection sounds like abjection and dejection. This is possibly no accident, since these are precisely the kinds of emotions that accompany a rejection. The writer feels as if they, not just their article, are not good enough. Nowhere is the knot of text work/identity work more apparent and more at risk than when the article is sent back with no option to change it. The decision is final. There is no way to retrieve it. It's a red card.

First of all, it's important to understand why articles are rejected. Graham Hobbs, the Editorial Director of the publisher Taylor and Francis, gives as his top ten reasons for rejection:

1. Sent to the wrong journal, does not fit the journal's aims and scope
2. Not a proper journal article (i.e. too journalistic, or clearly a thesis chapter, or a consultancy report)
3. Too long (ignoring word limits for the particular journal) or too short
4. Poor regard to the conventions of the journal (failure to consult Notes for Contributors) or to conventions of academic writing generally
5. Bad style, grammar, punctuation; poor English (not corrected by native speaker)

6. Fails to say anything of significance (i.e. makes no new contribution to the subject) or states the obvious at tedious length
7. Not properly contextualised (e.g. concentrates on parochial interests and ignores the needs of an international or generally wider readership)
8. No theoretical framework (including references to relevant literature)
9. Scrappily presented and clearly not proofread
10. Libellous, unethical, rude.

When we read this list we are struck by the number of points that relate to the layer 2/3 concerns we introduced in Chapter 2. Points 1, 2, 3 and 4 refer to the specific journal and the failure to attend to its conventions and guidelines. Points 6, 7 and 8 are concerned with the wider discourse community and the relevance and significance (or So what) of the article more broadly.

The reasons given by Hobbs for rejection resonate with those offered by many scholars responsible for journals. One of the most common reasons given by academic journal editors for rejection is that the authors sound like 'newbies' (Yates, 2004). Anthony Paré, editor of the *McGill Journal of Education*, observes wryly:

> As a journal Editor I now receive an increasing number of submissions from graduate students intent on publishing their 200-page dissertation as 15-page articles. It is rarely difficult to identify the authors as doctoral students. The topics are far too broad for short papers, the research methodologies are extensive and longitudinal, the theoretical terminology is impenetrable, the parentheses are crammed with citations, and the reference list is half as long as the paper itself. In other words, the submissions are reasonable facsimiles of student or school genres, but ineffective journal articles. They display knowledge . . . but fail to address an actual dialogue among working scholars.
>
> (Paré, 2010: 30)

Paré argues that early career writers cannot yet tell the difference between the texts required for assessment by examiners, and the kinds of texts deemed acceptable by referees and editors. Assignments, essays and theses typically need to provide evidence and audit trails that demonstrate that they use key processes and concepts. Each of these markers garners 'points' when submitted for assessment purposes. Leaving out the appropriate quantum of knowledge may lead to outright failure. This is not the case in journal articles where, as Paré notes, putting *in* this display of knowledge may well lead to rejection.

Another key reason nominated by academic editors for articles being rejected is that they lack focus (Wellington, 2003). The writer attempts to say 'everything', thereby focussing on 'nothing'. They succumb to the temptation to compress all of their 'thesis' or research into one article, whereas most good articles have one or two key ideas and these are worked thoroughly into a convincing case for scholarly attention.

Equally problematic is the failure to locate the contribution and the position – for a particular audience, in relation to wider debates and/or the specific conversation in the target journal. A further common problem is that the point the writer is trying to make is not significant – it's too local, it's been done a lot, it doesn't add anything, it doesn't offer a new 'angle'. These reasons are all related to the layer 2 and 3 interests and expectations of the specific journal discourse community.

An example of what we mean by 'no angle' comes from the *Educational Action Research Journal*. This is not an education journal as might be suggested by its name, but one which publishes action research in education, health, social care, youth and community work, and business. One of the practices inherent to action research is reflection, and this is where the 'education' comes from, because the researcher learns as they go along through formal processes of reflecting. In the twenty years of the journal's operation, there has probably been at least one article in each of the four issues per year which addresses reflection. So submitting an article on reflection to EARJ is sensible because it is something that readers are interested in and continue to be interested in. However, writers must have something *new* to say. There is no point simply offering a case which argues that reflection is useful. That's been said and done and that is why the journal exists. Writers for EARJ must not only take account of what's been said in the past, but also offer something different that adds to the conversation. However, EARJ editors report (and Pat is one) that they still receive a lot of submitted articles where writers do not seem to understand that they must take a new angle on reflection, they must offer something new to the field.

Interviews with journal editors on the Taylor and Francis Education Arena website (www.educationarena.com/expertinterviews/) highlight this same range of issues. They not only discuss layer 3, but also layer 2. Editors even say that they deal with a significant number of articles that have clearly been sent to the wrong journal. These are sent back without being reviewed simply because they do not meet the most basic requirement of the journal. It is as if writers have chosen the journal by title rather than from an understanding of the actual mission or methodology or field.

So what to do when the rejection letter is received, aside from learning from the specific feedback and the more general points we have outlined?

Of course it's OK to cry, swear, throw things around and crawl into the bottom drawer with the article, but only for a little while. One rejection doesn't mean that the writer should now give up. The task is to take on board the concerns and criticisms and to continue trying to get into the scholarly conversation.

Because we know how devastating rejection is, we always advise early career writers to target one journal but also, at the same time, to seriously select an appropriate alternative journal. Then, if the article is rejected, it *can* and *should* be revised in light of comments received and sent out again to the alternative publication. We talk later about the role of publication brokers and their role in supporting the rewriting.

Some people have even sent rejected articles out completely unchanged to another journal and had them accepted. But this is a risky strategy as the article may well go to the same reviewers, because most academics review for more than one journal. It's not something we'd do ourselves.

Revise and resubmit, or, one more time with feeling

While the rejection letter is final, the revise and resubmit offers the opportunity to try again. It's easy to focus on the negative in revise and resubmit letters. Some reviewer comments can be quite insensitive and wounding to scholarly identities in the making.

Welcome to the jungle. There is no tree to hide behind! The text is now in plain sight. In contrast to reality television programs where aspirant actors and models face daily critique and even ridicule, such direct evaluation is not the life experience of most academics. In fact, this is one of the relatively few times when the scholar is not in some way sheltered. Most of us in the academy are relatively protected from scrutiny and invective. The reception of our text is one of the times when we are visible – and vulnerable.

Many early career researchers are particularly unprepared for the brutality of the review process. The PhD process is often one which has been designed as a pedagogy of positivity. There is liberal praise as well as guidance and some critique. Good supervisors understand that at this stage a scholarly identity is emergent rather than fully formed. Care is generally taken to provide a lot of support and scaffolding. Most examiners read the PhD thesis as the work of a new scholar and their remarks are formative and appreciative, even when they ask for corrections. Journal reviewers, on the other hand, expect the writer to be an equal.

So when the letter advising revise and resubmit arrives there are three things to remember.

(1) Don't dash off a furious email to the editor

Telling the editor that they and the reviewers are idiots isn't the way to go. As Jonsson (2006: 482), a former editor of the *Scandinavian Journal of Management*, puts it:

> As editor I sometimes get letters from authors who are very angry with incompetent reviewers who have not even understood the simplest propositions. My answer is if friendly reviewers, who have volunteered to spend part of their busy life on this manuscript, and who are chosen because they are experts in the area, misunderstand, then there just might be something wrong with the way things are presented in the manuscript. In 90 per cent of the cases the fault is with the author and her or his way of expressing thoughts. It is childish to take offence from the reviewers. They do an important job and if they do not get the message try another way of formulating the text. This is the chance you get to have professional feedback based on the text alone (in blind review journals), not on friendship or respect or animosity. Use it to your own advantage rather than spend energy on cursing reviewers.

So find a close friend and spew out the invective and then . . .

(2) Deal with the negative commentary

A revise and resubmit means that the journal *is* interested in the writing and will publish if the work is done. A revise and resubmit is a conditional invitation to be part of the conversation of the journal. Jonsson again:

> The first thing to note in this situation is that the decision 'revise and resubmit' establishes a new bond between author and editor (and reviewers) because there is a common wish toward improvement. In spite of all the critical points raised the revise decision puts you in a very good position. Do not waste it by interpreting reviewer comments as hostile!
>
> (Jonsson, 2006: 488)

In other words, while there is no guarantee, the door is not closed. And . . .

(3) Hurry up

Don't put it off until tomorrow, because that means it's the bottom of the priority list. It's difficult, but it's one more time with feeling *now*.

Waiting too long to send an article back breaks the bond between editor and writer and creates more work for reviewers. It misunderstands the nature of the contract – it is not only revise but also resubmit. This does not mean either waiting for months, nor does it mean sending it back overnight in a desperate attempt to get rid of it. Revision means timely reconsideration of the text. Editors often specify a given time period, perhaps three months. If this is ignored the resubmission will be treated as if it's new, and the process will start all over again.

One way for early career researchers to manage the revision process is with a publication broker.

Publication brokers

Publication brokering is the term we use to mark the essential work of mediating the revise and resubmit process (see also Kamler, 2010). Complex and difficult decisions need to be made about how to address reviewer comments in terms of the disciplinary knowledge, debates, structural framing and the discourses of the target journal. Publication brokering can be done by a variety of people – supervisors, colleagues, writing mates, writing groups and other academic professionals. In Chapter 9 we discuss working with writing mates and writing groups, to help bring a text to the point of submission. They may also become publication brokers after the review is received, but the writer may equally choose someone else.

Recent theorising on the central role of brokers comes from Lillis and Curry (2006, 2010) who use the term *literacy brokers*. In their research with multilingual scholars who are seeking publication in international English-medium journals, they include as literacy brokers all the people who impact directly on helping texts get published. These might include editors, reviewers, academic professionals and academic peers, linguistic professionals, English-speaking friends and colleagues. Lillis and Curry argue that brokering activity uses and generates a form of cultural capital that makes a critical difference to publication outcomes. Access to brokers can ensure publication; enhance the prestige and reputation of writers; and also secure more direct forms of economic gain, such as promotion and salary bonuses.

Lillis and Curry draw attention to the significance of publication brokers, particularly for writers who use English as an Additional Language. There is now pressure from many governments for scholars to publish in English and there are in some places diminishing numbers of first language journals. In these circumstances increasing numbers of multilingual scholars are turning to English language specialists – proofreaders, editors and the like – to assist with the technicalities of expression. A greater number access academic brokers who often combine language support with disciplinary expertise. Such brokerage is important for publication but remains relatively under-researched. Lillis and Curry's book is an important contribution to understanding not only what these brokers do, but also their uneven distribution across the globe.

We use the term brokering more narrowly than Lillis and Curry to describe interactions that occur after the article is returned. We are thinking of the broker as a trusted senior colleague to whom the early career writer can turn, article and reviewer comments in hand.

Clearly newcomers find the resubmission process complex, troublesome and difficult to interpret. Publication brokers can help bruised and worried writers interpret what is happening in the social, cultural and political climate of revise and resubmit so they can take effective textual action. Conversations with brokers about the content of an article and the broader (layer 3) disciplinary conventions and journal conventions (layer 2) play a critical role in successful publication.

Publication brokering is obviously useful for doctoral researchers new to the game. We think, for example, of a doctoral researcher named Sam who was so devastated by negative reviewer comments that she decided not to resubmit (see Lee and Kamler, 2008). Admittedly, the criticism of her methodological work was harshly stated. One reviewer said: 'I would consequently question if this new format is indeed in any way innovative or new on the dimensions that the paper claims. I find this to be a major flaw in the research reported within the paper'. Sam was so upset by this commentary that she didn't read the letter from the editor, which asked her to revise and return the revised manuscript within 30 days.

It was not until she brought the letter to her supervisor that she understood. Despite the stated problems, the editor *wanted* her article. '30 days' signalled there was a publication deadline the editor needed to meet. The editor thought the problems in Sam's article were 'fixable'; the supervisor thought so too. There was no purpose in crying for too long. Sam actually knew the literature far better than she demonstrated in the article and had to work hard to show why and how her contribution was different from previous work – why it was *new*. Without the input of her supervisor to broker the revision process, she would not have resubmitted. What a wasted opportunity that would have been!

We can see how crucial the role of brokering is in a further example, that of Thomas. Thomas completed a PhD by publication. He was required to write three articles and an exegesis, all of these in English; his first language is Norwegian. His PhD depended on having the three articles accepted for publication. This mode of PhD is becoming increasingly common across Europe (Lee, 2010) and is argued to be more internationally oriented as well as preparing students better for the current realities of being a scholar.

Thomas's first article took two years from initial submission to final publication. During that time he had to make major revisions to it. His second article was accepted with minor revisions. His third article was rejected and had to be submitted to another journal altogether. But in the first and third articles there were conflicting reviews and an extended set of exchanges with reviewers and editors over many months. At times Thomas did not know whether he would meet the requirements for his PhD because of the level of critical comments he received. The time lapse and prolonged nature of revising and resubmitting, then revising again and resubmitting again, were extremely challenging. Thomas says:

> The nature of blind reviewing implies that the candidate receives the same level of feedback as is given to experienced scholars. The critiques of the reviewers and editors often appear frank and direct, which can be difficult and even destructive in the fragile course of learning for an inexperienced scholar. The role of the supervisor is crucial in helping the PhD candidate interpret and digest the feedback in order to make the comments beneficial and help the candidate revise his or her work.
>
> (De Lange, 2011)

Such high-stakes publishing for a PhD raises the bar on the riskiness and importance of publication. Early career and doctoral researchers are highly dependent in these situations, not only on their supervisors as brokers, but on skilful editors to lead them through a difficult review process.

Editors as publication brokers

Many editors recognise the complex, sometimes hostile and contradictory advice offered in reviewer reports (Kamler, 2010; Murray, 2005; Wellington, 2003). Good editors understand that they need to guide authors about how to negotiate harsh and conflicting reviewer demands. They take an active role in synthesizing and giving direction – which advice to attend to fully, which to background, perhaps which to ignore.

Thomas, whom we introduced above, describes the critical role of the editor in brokering his third article. The editor received two conflicting reviews and then asked the reviewers to sort out their differences.

> The editor described the disagreement and also attached the follow up discussion that occurred between the reviewers. The most interesting part of this is *how* the editor conveyed his message. First of all, he displayed the grounds of the rejection, preparing me for the frankness of the reviewers'

statements and thoroughly explained the considerations an editor needed to account for. The editor also made an effort to motivate me to continue my research and invited me to submit to the journal again. In this sense, the rejection gave me, as a PhD student, valuable insights into the review and editorial process.

(De Lange, 2011)

This editorial intervention is quite unusual. It is rare to ask reviewers to resolve their differences. However, this gave Thomas the opportunity to see a dialogue between scholars with different positions as they discussed his work and then came to an agreement about what would be required to bring it to publishable standards. It is more common for the editor to do this work – deciding which review recommendations to prioritise.

Form letters from editors, asking writers to simply attend to reviewer comments and return the manuscript showing the changes made, seriously if unwittingly misrepresent what's at stake for the writer. Revise and resubmit entails complex discursive, social and emotional work that needs expert mediation from a variety of academic players, editors included. There is too much to learn and too much at stake for most early career writers to do this work alone.

Good editors are self-conscious about the partial and sometimes contradictory nature of reviewer reports and the need to mediate these for authors. One editor says:

So, in some cases it seems to me that our job as editors is to help articulate the confusion, under writing, under reporting, or inadequacy of the study indexed by the reviewers' comments. But, in other cases it seems to me our task is to articulate the differing epistemological and ontological positions of the reviewers . . . Thus, it does not seem appropriate for an editor to merely pass the reviewers' comments on to the author without framing them and incorporating them into a coherent response from the editors.

(Personal communication with editor in Kamler 2010: 72)

Even if editors do this work, and they don't always, early career writers can still benefit from additional brokerage in making sense of what reviewers want. We want now, however, to say a bit more about working out what the reviewers and editors actually want us to do when revising.

Learning to read the reviewers

When writers receive reviewer comments we may not yet know the journal codes and often wonder: What do they mean? However, when we read real estate ads, we understand that there is a code. 'Renovation potential' means it's a dump. 'First home buyers' dream' means it's a dump. 'Original condition' means it's a dump.

Journal reviewers usually have their own codes, but these are not uniform across discourse communities, let alone disciplines. Each reviewer has idio-syncratic ways of telling the writer what to do. And, just like writers, reviewers don't always quite know what they are trying to say. At times, they know there is a problem, but they can't put their finger on it. So they have a stab at saying what they think is going on and it is not always clear what action might resolve the problem.

Let us illustrate what we mean by coded reviewer comments. Take these excerpts from two reviewer reports:

> Reviewer 1: Perhaps it might be helpful to explore the conceptual and theoretical issues around identity and how that links to the issues around power in much more depth.

> Reviewer 2: The theoretical approach brings together roles, identity and habitus as if these were commensurate concepts. Identity is not anchored to any theoretical paradigm, Bourdieu is given pretty short shrift and the potential of field theory is not explored. Role theory is used most in the paper even though it could be explicated more fully. One of these approaches needs to be adopted and explicated in detail.

Reviewer 2 is more direct and more specific. Although both reviewers say much the same thing, the writer might have a better idea about what to do from Reviewer 2's comments.

What is implied in both comments is that the writer's take on identity is confused, perhaps even simplistic and facile. Neither of the reviewers has been rude, but it would be a mistake to read these comments as minor. Reviewer 1 says 'more depth' while reviewer 2 says 'in detail'. Both are code for requiring substantial rethinking and rewriting. This is not about a paragraph or a few more references. This is a fundamental reworking of the theoretical basis of the argument.

This is just one example of the need to decode and read below the surface of reviewer comments.

Decoding may be a significant issue for EAL writers because codes cannot be literally translated – they must be interpreted using cultural knowledges. Rottier *et al.* (2011) address common communication problems between English and Dutch medical practitioners, and include in their discussion clarification about some expressions often used in journal reviews. They say, for example, that when the British say/write 'I would suggest' this actually means it is a requirement, but that Dutch readers would understand this phrase as an option. Similarly, when the British say/write 'Perhaps you could give more thought to' they actually mean to take a different course of action, whereas the Dutch reader interprets this as meaning that they should consider potential problems. While these kinds of cultural stereotypical lists can be amusing, there is a serious point made here, that understanding what reviewers say is rarely a matter of literal reading – it is always a reading between the lines and this takes layer 2/3 knowledges. Reid (2010) specifically addresses these cultural issues in her book *Getting published in international journals: Writing strategies for European social scientists.*

Because reading a review is always difficult, brokers who are experienced writers themselves are invaluable in interpreting revise and resubmit letters. They can assist the writer to sort out what is being said, whether the comments are being polite, a bit confused, culturally loaded or using euphemisms.

Some of the texts on writing for publication are also helpful here. They give students a feel for the complexities and politics of peer review, rather than simply treating the process procedurally or neutrally. Murray (2005) in *Writing for academic journals* offers a variety of reviewer comments – showing both destructive and encouraging feedback – and how to deal with hostile reviews. Wellington (2003) in *Getting published: A guide for lecturers and researchers* does similar work in making explicit the kinds of critical commentary authors can expect from reviewers. However, he also asks, Why do we subject people to peer review? His interviews with twelve editors of education journals illuminate the contested conversations about the drawbacks as well as the benefits of the peer review system.

Of course, simply understanding the reviewer comments is not enough. There is always a choice about how to respond, about what to do. Writers can decide which or any or all of the reviewer comments they will attend to. Many writers, particularly if they're new, think that they have to follow each and every recommendation slavishly. If there are points of disagreement between reviewers that the editor has not clarified, then there is an obvious choice to be made. The writer can't please everyone. If there is strong editorial guidance about what to do, the writer is taking a risk in deciding not to follow, especially as the article will most likely be sent back to the same referees. So if the choice is made not to do what they say, it has to be argued.

Keeping the integrity of the argument and the article is of paramount concern. Reviewers often go off on a tangent; they see something interesting that may not be germane to the main argument. In this instance, the writer may need to say 'I've made a note that this is a potential area to be explored, but not now'. At other times reviewers may make suggestions that disrupt the flow of the article or add unduly to the word length.

We often observe early career writers treating reviewer reports as a set of exam questions to be answered. One writer we know, for example, was critiqued for not showing the significance of her research to the field. Her solution was to insert two pages of additional literature work to show other scholars also addressing her research problem. The result was a mess. Her paper lost focus and balance. She answered the reviewer diligently and methodically, but at the expense of her own argument. A broker helped her reduce these two pages to one paragraph and acknowledge the point within reason.

It is important to remember that reviewer comments happen off-stage (de Lauretis, 1987). They are, however, vital to the progress of the publication, even though none of the evaluative work that goes on behind the scenes is visible to the readers of the final paper (Fortanet, 2008). Reviewer and editor comments are the backstory to the final performance – which is the published article. This actual performance must be coherent and stand on its own. We can't let what happens backstage ruin the production. The writer must keep their eye on their own purposes, attend to reviewers, but not slavishly. Brokers can play an important role in this complex decision-making process.

Writing the letter back

Having negotiated the reviewers' concerns (hard work) and decided which changes to make, the writer has to communicate these decisions (even harder) to the editor. Writers are often advised to simply be polite and tell the editor exactly what they've done.

This is more than a technical exercise of compliance or documenting changes. It is a textual site of identity work for the emerging scholar, presenting the scholarly self and her revised text to the discourse community for recon-sideration. Acceptance is not a given. What discursive stance might be appro-priate for telling a more powerful editor how reviewer advice has been followed, or not?

Writing back to the editor is what is called an occluded text – one of those invisible academic genres that are rarely shown and treated as a minor event (Swales, 1990). The work that is required to construct these texts is assumed, but rarely made explicit. They can thus remain something of a mystery to the novice writer.

Barbara (Kamler, 2010) has analysed letters written to editors by differently positioned scholars: an inexperienced doctoral writer and two more experienced co-authors, one pair dealing with fairly straightforward critique; the other with a lengthy and difficult set of demands over a protracted period of time. The continuum of response she shows suggests the discursive stance most often taken by writers is shaped by their experience, confidence and status in the field.

However, regardless of seniority, there really is no need for diffidence. The editor is the representative of the discourse community and the revising writer has to adopt an appropriate combination of authoritativeness and politeness when in conversation with them. They must speak like a member of the community in their response. This is peer-to-peer talk. And a publication broker can help all writers, regardless of their seniority, respond confidently and articulately to revise and resubmit requirements.

The following example was written by Barbara in 2008 to the editor of *Studies in Higher Education*. Her article 'Rethinking doctoral publication practices: Writing from and beyond the thesis' examined a case study of doctoral graduates in science and education (discussed in Chapter 8) to show how the practices of each discourse community affected student publication. Her argument in the article was that co-authorship with supervisors significantly enhanced the robustness and know-how of emergent scholars, as well as their publication output.

Barbara's opening was courteous without being obsequious.

> Thank you for the opportunity to interact with the reviewer reports on my article and to revise accordingly. While both reviews were, as you say, generally positive, there seemed to be two key concerns that I overlooked and have now addressed.

Here, Barbara has acknowledged there were problems in the article, but said that she has addressed them. She responds to the critique by synthesising the reviewer commentary into two major and one minor point. This is quite different than slavishly replying point by point to reviewer comments or making track changes as if revising is a mechanical matter of simply inserting the answers to the questions reviewers ask. Here is her first point.

> I summarise these as follows:

> My assumption about the importance of doctoral publication. Reviewer 2 asks 'does it really matter that PhD students don't publish' and seems to imply a publish for publish sake argument in my writing. Reviewer 1 suggests there are some who see publishing during candidature as an impediment to writing a thesis and that I don't consider the downside of publishing.

After this, Barbara then goes on to refute these criticisms and to argue for her position, thereby justifying the changes she made to the text.

I have strong feelings about the importance of doctoral publishing, but believe I may have not argued the case strongly enough in this article. To address this absence, I have revamped, in particular, the introduction and used the research of McGrail (as reviewer 1 suggests) not just to reiterate the lack of publishing in the past, BUT to suggest that if we wish to change this pattern, we need to look more critically at how our own pedagogic practices produce a non-publishing culture. And doctoral education is a good place to start if we wish, as Golde and Walker (2006) argue, to produce 'stewards of the discipline'. One has to ask, if the results of research are not published, then really what is the point? In the conclusion, I have added commentary to argue that publication can take the work of the thesis forward – not simply act as an impediment. I include a new example from the study of a student who did not publish – and deeply regretted this – to highlight that even students who do not take on academic careers can benefit from engaging in international journal dialogue with peers. This example is briefly inserted so as not to increase the length too much.

The second point follows the same pattern. Barbara presents her version of the reviewers' critique about her sample comparability, indicates the moves she's made to redress the problem and then restates her argument. Here we have put in bold the skeleton of rhetorical moves being made.

I agree that this information was under-presented in the article and have addressed this by revamping the second section of the paper entitled *The research context*. **I have made more explicit** the rationale for selecting the cohorts, why Education was selected in relation to the composition of the research team. **I explain that the aim is not to** compare disciplines, and that this would be impossible, as reviewer 1 suggests. **Rather it is to** compare pedagogic practices by seeing their effects on student capacity to publish. **I highlight** the different experiences of students with regard to patterns of candidature (e.g. full time vs part time, mid vs early career). **The reviewer commentary made me aware of** how much 'taken for granted' information remained implicit.

Barbara then clarifies exactly what her intention is and hints that she thinks the reviewers may not have understood the distinction she is making between discipline and discourse community. We have bolded the meta-commentary to show how she makes her argument quite clear.

I not only explicitly state that the aim is not to compare disciplines, but delete language that seems to overgeneralise (as reviewer 2 notes). **I**

emphasise that I am looking at the impact of pedagogic practice in different *discourse communities* not just in disciplines. **This is a fine distinction, perhaps, but one that is in line with** the theoretical framing of my research and its treatment of doctoral writing as a discursive social practice. From this lens, differences in student publication and output are seen as produced in these communities and thus can be made differently.

This is not simply responding to critique, but continuing to argue for the article and its significance.

I have also revamped the conclusion and added a new reference to Golde and Walker (2006) **to make this point more strongly and to again stress that I am not interested in** publication for publication's sake – or for boosting the RAE or the like. **Rather, it is important to** create structures in our disciplines that enable students to participate – as it is these structures, as McGrail et al point out, that make a difference to whether academics publish or not. **If they do** so in their formative years, they are **more likely to** do so as established academics or informed professionals in their chosen fields of practice.

This letter to the editor is an argument through and through. We have cited it at length and highlighted the meta-commentary to make the point that such letters rarely just report on the revisions that have been made. They can be complex arguments that *negotiate critique, answer back,* and *provide continued justification for decisions made.* The tone here is forthright, but it is still arguing for acceptance.

What is not evident in this letter (Barbara hopes) is her initial temper tantrum when she read the reviewer reports. This was a difficult article to write. She had given five conference papers on the study, making multiple arguments. Getting the argument clear for this article was confusing and Barbara struggled to use detail from the empirical work without overgeneralising. The reviewer requests, in particular those referred to in point two, seemed too hard to deal with. So Barbara conferred with a close colleague, who brokered her resubmission and helped her condense the critique into the two major points and thus make it doable.

The point we wish to make is that engaging critique is difficult – no matter how experienced the writer. Brokers can play a critical role to help the writer gain distance, strategise, deal with confusing or conflicting reviewer advice and read critically the resulting revision. In the immediate absence of a broker, writers might consult Murray (2005) and Belcher (2009).

So what, now what?

The euphoria of being published is worth celebrating. The elated scholar must take a moment to savour the moment and the marker of success. As a participant in one of Barbara's writing groups put it:

> Actually going through this process and plugging away and plugging away and getting the article back and it saying this needs to be done and going through the process again. And then getting the final 'yes it's been accepted' was 'oh my God!', it's very exciting. That confidence that you get from one part of your work translates into other parts and that tends to build. I've been through this process, now I know what else to do. So it's resilience building.
>
> (Personal communication with participant, unpublished)

The textual experience of getting published impacts on scholarly identity in a positive way. The words and the self are out there in the community. The scholar is now part of the conversation.

But – isn't there always a but! – identity formation is not a simple process, it's not a once in a career happening. Sending the article back and seeing it in print is not the end of the story. One journal article leads to another. And, increasingly, articles are written with other scholars, both emerging and experienced. In the next chapter we address writing with others and how collaborative work can build networks, reputation and identities as well as texts.

Chapter 8

Writing with others

In the last seven chapters we have looked at the ways in which a single reviewed journal article can be developed and refined. We have introduced and used our key concepts – layers 1, 2 and 3; text work/identity work, and making a contribution to discourse communities – to introduce a number of strategies which writers can use to guide and focus their efforts as they craft the scholarly paper and deal with critique. In this chapter we want to change our focus to collaborative writing.

Working with others to *compose* and *construct* our text is an integral part of the process of building a scholarly career and writing portfolio. This writing may be with one other person or more, so that we can distinguish between co-writing and team writing. But no matter how many people are involved, the text is being made collaboratively, and its making does not rest on our shoulders alone.

But why work with others? Whether working in a higher education institution or as a social researcher in the private, third or public sector, scholars now increasingly work in teams. The popular imaginary may still be of one writer working alone, doing the research and writing about it. If this ever was the case, it is changing now. It is common for social science researchers to work and write together, just as in the 'hard' sciences. Working collaboratively, evidenced in joint publications, is now more highly valued by promotion panels and tenure committees. It is de rigueur for work outside the academy, where job descriptions invariably ask for evidence of the ability to work cooperatively and collaboratively. Even in the most elite universities, the early career singleton unable to demonstrate that they can work together with others is just as likely to be regarded with some suspicion as with admiration. Thinking about how writing together is integral to contemporary scholarship is thus very important.

Writing together

We get asked a lot of questions about collaboration and how we manage to do it. We also see a great deal of early career researcher fear and desire emanating from the very idea of working with someone else. Early scholars are often afraid that their hard-won intellectual property will be taken and claimed. They feel vulnerable about making their writing practices visible to their writing partners. They feel uncomfortable about managing the power relations with more senior colleagues – how will they tell them if the work is not good?

Collaboration is classic text work/identity work. The writer is manoeuvring and managing both at the same time, when they may not feel at all confident about themselves, let alone the other person. Early career researchers face the challenge of developing a 'signature' in and through their writing. They must, as we explained in Chapter 2, use their writing to build an agenda that they will be known for. They also become known for the clarity, elegance and/or engaging nature of their writing. When writing with others, this emerging identity and signature may be swamped or obliterated – or it may be enhanced. These are real concerns.

In this chapter we consider the views of more experienced writers in order to tease out what is involved in this kind of collaborative work. We examine why people do it, why they like it and how they manage. We address the issues that arise when doctoral researchers write with their supervisors. First we begin by outlining our understanding of collaborative writing.

Types of collaborative writing

There are a number of ways to think about collaboration. We have seen, for example, an argument which suggests that citing the work of others is a form of collaboration. While we can see this point, we think that this is not helpful to a discussion of academic writing practice. Using other people's work is not the same as composing text together and it is this latter process that most of us mean when we talk about collaborative writing.

We propose three types of writing collaboration:

(1) Type-talk: where two or more people sit side by side at the computer and write together
(2) Cut it up and put it back together: where two or more people divide the paper into sections and write these separately, then one person puts the draft together
(3) First cut: where one person takes the lead and writes the first draft in its entirety and the others add, subtract and amend.

We know that this is not the only way to describe these kinds of collaborations. For example, we have recently come across a blog post by Tseen Khoo (http://www.theresearchwhisperer.wordpress.com) which describes: *layering*, where one person does a first draft and team members make serial alterations, *bricolage*, where research team members are allocated sections to write, and *lego*, where the team jointly work out the paper and its structure and then write pieces which the leader stitches together. However, we will use the labels (1)–(3) above as they seem to us to describe the process more explicitly.

In order to help us think about co-writing, we recently invited a number of well-known and highly respected education academics with long-standing writing partnerships to reflect with us on the question of how and why they write together. Michelle Fine and Lois Weis have written numerous books and articles together including *The unknown city: Lives of poor and working class young adults* (1998); *Speed bumps: A student-friendly guide to qualitative research* (2000); and *Silenced voices and extraordinary conversation: Reimagining schools* (2003). Fazal Rizvi and Bob Lingard have co-authored numerous texts including *Globalising education policy* (Rivzi and Lingard, 2009) and with Miriam Henry and Sandra Taylor *Education policy and the politics of change* (S. Taylor *et al.*, 1997). Michael Peters has written over 35 books and 300 articles; he is often thought of in connection with long time co-author Jim Marshall. His collaborations include *Wittgenstein: Philosophy, postmodernism, pedagogy* (Peters and Marshall, 1999); *Subjectivity and truth: Foucault, education, and the culture of the self* (Peters and Besley, 2007) and *Creativity and the global knowledge economy* (Peters *et al.*, 2008). Gary Anderson and Kathryn Herr have co-written several articles and two books *The action research dissertation: A guide for students and faculty* (Herr and Anderson, 2005) and *Studying your own school: An educator's guide to practitioner action research* (Anderson *et al.*, 2008).

Our interview analysis showed there was not one way of co-writing. Successful partners seem to use the three ways we have outlined for composing together. We now consider each of the three in more detail using quotations from interviews to reveal what the approach actually entails.

Type-talk strategy

In this form of collaboration writing is an extension of talk and the relationship between the writers. Ongoing dialogue is central, it fuels the writing. In the talking there is a sense of discovering things together. The talking spills onto the page with the co-writers taking turns to do the actual keyboard work. Michael Peters describes working with Jim Marshall in this way:

> We took turns. Someone would sit at the typewriter and then someone would dictate. It was an equal share of the actual physical process of doing

the typing and the talking and sometimes it would break off and we would
have the discussion.

Type-talk requires time and space together. It relies on trust and being in
tune with one another. Fazal Rizvi notes that this approach requires an
openness, but that trust is built further through the writing. It grows over time.
He says of his collaboration with Steven Kemmis:

> We loved writing together. We did a number of things together where we
> would just be sitting there and he would be typing away as I am dictating
> and then he would dictate and I would type and sometimes there would
> be a struggle for the mouse. The struggle for the mouse became a kind of
> metaphor (for the way we interacted).

This is also how Barbara and Pat work together. We live in different parts of
the world and must build type-talk time into our working year. The first part
of this book was written in Singapore and the second in Melbourne. Without
this time together to talk-type, we find we can write bits of chapters, but cannot
do the cohesive conceptual work which relies on our face-to-face dialogue.

Cut it up and put it back together

This is quite a different process, although it still floats on talk. There is initial
discussion about the ideas and the concepts and how these should be developed
in the paper. But then the sections of an article are split up. Decisions are jointly
made about who will be responsible for which sections. Each writer works
independently and then the text is melded together. Bob Lingard explains how
this process works when he and Fazal write together:

> What Fazal and I tend to do is we will talk a lot – particularly if it's a book,
> we will talk a lot about the structure and we tend to write down the
> structure and Fazal often also says that we'll have this many words on this
> script and then we'll have this many on this and then we'll each write a
> section and then one of us will write in the connections.

In order for this approach to work, there has to be a common ground
between the writers. Trust is required that each person will do their part – and
on time – and when this does not occur tensions can emerge. Separately or
together, the writers must work to *write over* the text so it becomes a unified
voice rather then a duet or a chorus. Refining and editing the text requires an
agreed set of decisions. This can be challenging as we discuss later in this section.

This approach can be a very good strategy for early career researchers. In fact, Pat learned to write an academic article in exactly this way, thanks to her colleague Alan Reid. She had been used to writing short stories and journalistic articles but the journal article was a new genre. Cutting it up and putting it back together was a good way to learn how to structure an argument and to think about the order and flow of the chunks.

First cut

In this approach, one partner takes the lead to write the first draft, then passes it to the other partner(s) for refining and revision. Progressive drafts are passed back and forth.

Michelle Fine and Lois Weis do most of their writing in this way:

> Someone does the first cut and we don't talk too much about it because we don't have the time. Someone does the first cut and then the cut goes to the next person and then the person will write and rewrite and revise. With *Unknown City* we had to think through: can we develop a method that draws on the theoretical and critical skills that we each bring to be able to think about structure; track ideology but then do ethnography as well and our working method comes right out of that . . . So somebody would do the first draft and we'd rewrite it and we would spend a lot of time with *Unknown City* reading the data and saying: how do we make sense of it?

Conversation is still essential to the first cut working, but it occurs at a different time. It is a relational, political and conversational approach rather than simply one of efficiency. However, the conversation is built on trust and there must be little ego involved when work is being written over and remade.

Although not all writers share the intimacy of Fine and Weis, this is the way that many research teams work. Someone takes the lead and then the others chip in. Sometimes the group might carve out pieces for each person to do, either working to their strengths and knowledge, or simply making allocations on an arbitrary basis. This can work very well. But if the power relations in the group haven't been discussed or are unresolved, then this approach can lead to quarrels, bitterness and ongoing and deep resentments. There needs to be adequate discussion about what is to be done as well as the procedure, who will do what when, and how difficulties will be resolved. Some research teams develop an authorship protocol at the beginning of research projects in order to avoid just these problems (see later in this chapter).

We now look in greater depth at these collaborative relationships.

What makes these collaborations work?

From our interviews with experienced writers we identified four key characteristics of successful collaborations.

(1) Collaborators develop strong personal relationships

Our interviewees all liked each other. They often used family metaphors to describe one another, as sisters, brothers. Michelle Fine told us:

> We came together with a sensibility about the work and how it should be done and then our relationship, like really good bread that rises, developed these layers around children and lives and humour and politics and work and grants and books. And it's certainly been my oxygen. For me it felt like we were separated at birth, you know. I didn't have a buddy and I didn't even know I wanted one but then I thought to be able to have an intellectual friend and a political ally in the academy is just a gift.

Fazal Rivzi noted:

> There has to be trust and there has to be politics. If there isn't then it is very difficult to write. The other thing that has to happen is conviviality and humour. Humour sustains us quite a lot because we are making mistakes all the time, so unless we can actually get over it through humour and not through criticism, then I think we are in trouble.

Michael Peters observed of his relationships with Jim Marshall:

> We knew each other and we were such good friends that it was very hard to wound each other even if we were brutally frank about ideas and about each other. Ultimately we were like extensions of each other.

We saw a distinctive kind of intimacy in the lasting writing collaborations. Gary Anderson and Kathryn Herr are married and their academic and personal relationships are knotted together in and through their joint writing.

> It's discussed over the kitchen table when we are swapping ideas or also if one of us is more passionate about something. I think a lot of the articles that we've done together have been the result of draconian deadlines, you know . . . like that Bourdieu work, for example, I came home and said that I'd committed us to writing this article so now what do we do? She had the data so we started theorising.

The words repeatedly used in our interviews were *trust, openness, talk*. These writing collaborators admire each other's work and, over the years, the writing became integral to a life-long friendship.

(2) Collaborators learn from each other

Our interviews show mutuality – a coming together that benefits both collaborators. While the time together is convivial, there is also something new created in the interchange, a complementarity brought about through an excitement in being stretched to see differently. This most often happens when co-writers come from slightly different disciplinary and/or theoretical lenses.

Michelle (psychologist) and Lois (sociologist) highlight the importance of reciprocity and learning from a partner with complementary skills. Lois says:

> Michelle stretches into psych in a way that I cannot manage. I talk about people's lives but my head just doesn't go into the interior mind. And Michelle stretches in that direction and I stretch quickly towards the economy and the social structures so it was really perfect. And the line that we put together was wholly different from the one that I would imagine that I would have put together and it was most productive because we had that extra dimension.

Fazal (philosopher) also reported learning from Bob (sociologist):

> Well the thing that I learnt from Bob is evidence. So how in the world does that abstract argument relate to the real world? I think he has given me materiality which is something that I didn't have before. Because I was trained as an analytical philosopher, arguments matter. The contents of those arguments could have been anything. I mean I was politically committed but my politics and my academic work were parallel to each other. But what Bob taught me was the fusion of my writing and my political beliefs and so, in that sense, my writing became much more political than it would have been otherwise.

We have similar kinds of disciplinary differences. Barbara is a sociolinguist and Pat is a sociologist. While it might seem like a cliché to say that the sum of this kind of collaboration is greater than the parts, it is, in our and our interviewees' cases, true.

John-Steiner (2000), who researched very famous research partnerships, notes that both difference and commonality matter in collaboration.

When individuals join together and build upon their complementarity in scientific disciplines, they expand their reach. The strength of these partnerships is as much in their common vision as in their complementary abilities. Collaboration offers partners an opportunity to transcend their individuality and to overcome the limitations of habit, and of biological and temporal constraints.

(John-Steiner, 2000: 57)

Her reference to 'common vision' holds true in our interviews where it is clear that learning from each other occurs because there are common commitments and imaginaries at work. Writing collaborations operate in an inter-subjective space where there is reciprocity of knowledge sharing, created through dialogue and text production.

(3) Collaborators support each other's identity work

One of the most obvious benefits that occurs in writing collaborations is support. Working with another person is a form of discipline. If one person is feeling hesitant then the other very often can take the lead. This involves more than simply motivation or discipline or comfort – although it is all of these. It is also a space within which the writers' identities are shaped and consolidated. Bob and Fazal explain:

> Bob: One of the things that writing with Fazal has meant for me is that it took me quite a long time to find my own voice as a writer. You would use everybody else's arguments rather than push your own argument in your work. And writing with Fazal has helped me change that because one of the things we always did was say that this is the main thread of our argument. So we would have an argument and it was our argument and we'd use other people just in reference. And maybe that's just a maturity and confidence thing but I know that writing with Fazal – because of his philosophical training which I don't have – I think that is a form of discipline and a strength for the writing which is really important. And I know that the first few times I wrote with Fazal I loved it and I was always the hesitant one. I was the one who wondered whether I could really stand up and say this. But now I don't feel that and that is one of the things that I got from Fazal.

> Fazal: I used to complain about that: why are you afraid? All you can do is get it wrong. Nobody is going to kill you over it. You might even be able to create debate. I think this is the difference in our backgrounds. I was brought up in an intellectual family where my father was writing all

the time and he modelled all that stuff so writing was no big deal and publishing was no big deal. That was just the family trade. My father was an academic, my grandfather was an academic and my great grandfather was an academic. So it's in my body and I never worried about things in the way that Bob did earlier on.

Writing partners often act as each other's safety net. They not only make the writing less lonely, they also provide encouragement for risk-taking and for doing the critical and assertive work necessary for authoritative scholarship. Pat and Barbara certainly find that if one of us is tentative, or even just out-of-sorts, the other can keep the momentum going. Together, we provide each other with the energy, focus and enthusiasm for our work and its value.

(4) Collaborators develop strategies for a unified voice

Collaborative writing always produces a challenge to make a unified voice from the different input. None of us thinks or writes in the same way. But the final text needs to look as though we do. This does not happen by accident and experienced collaborating writers know that hard labour is required to make this happen.

Sometimes writers formalise a structure for how this remoulding will go – especially when there are more than two authors. Fazal and Bob describe their approach with four people.

> Fazal: We had two people who did every chapter in the policy book – a different pair for each chapter – then when it was done the other two wrote over it – so that you can't really tell who wrote what, a group voice emerges.

> Bob: The *Leading Learning* book was very well planned and very well thought out and we used the same model as we did for the policy book: two people for each chapter and then we wrote back into them and I think we did the introduction collectively. What we did was use the data projector and we went away to a professional centre for three or four days and for the intro we wrote that collectively. We would write it and it would go up on the screen and we'd re-read it and talk about it. And I loved it. It was really interesting and I think we achieved an almost single voice through that collective writing onto the screen.

After doing this kind of process for a time, producing a common writing voice becomes as natural as writing separately. As Lois explained:

I could always get inside Michelle's head but I couldn't do that with anybody else. I could always get inside her argument and see where she is going with this and by the end we were really writing in tandem, although you could tell whose sentence that might be, it's not in a different voice. It really reads as if one person wrote it.

We find this too. In our first book (Kamler and Thomson, 2006) we spent a long time trying to sort out the tone, syntax, sentence structure and mode of address. Starting each chapter was a very time consuming process. These days it's much easier and we generally start writing without discussing any of the syntactical niceties. We think that we sound more like each other, even when we are not writing side by side.

The four strategies we have described are derived from conversations with long-standing academic writing partners. However, not all partnerships are as happy and fruitful as these.

When collaborations don't work

It is unfortunate that not all collaborations work out well. Things *can* go wrong. People don't pull their weight. People don't meet deadlines. They write really badly and it's hard to sort through the problems without feelings being damaged. People won't give up ideas, phrases, sentences, paragraphs because they are too attached to them. They are just not prepared to compromise in order to get the writing done. Every change seems to create a problem. Any of the above can cause conflicts which, at worst, stay unresolved.

The reality is that we can't write with everyone. The moral is that it is therefore vital to choose writing partners well. This means being selective. It's tempting to be overly grateful or flattered when someone asks to be our writing partner. It's equally tempting to ask someone to join in when the writing assignment is difficult or overwhelming. Barbara remembers how, early in her career, she was invited to contribute a chapter to a high profile book and was simply terrified. She decided to ask a colleague to co-author since they had already done research together. It was a disaster. The person did not produce text on time or meet deadlines and only contributed when Barbara threatened to write as a sole author. Suddenly text appeared, but it was different in style, undigested in its conceptualisation and not up to the job. It took twice as much work to massage the two sections together than if Barbara had done it all herself in the first place.

One solution would be speed dating for potential writing partners. We imagine ourselves sitting at a table with three minutes to interview a bevy of prospective writing partners. We fantasise about what we would ask:

How quickly do you write? Have you ever not met a deadline? What will you do if we have a disagreement? What do you think about alternating who is first author? What is your greatest weakness as a writer? Can you provide a reference from a previous co-author? Why and how did your last writing partnership end?

The politics of the academy may not allow us to say such things out loud, but the point is that whether we are choosing a writing partner for a one-night stand, or for a long-term relationship, the problems we have detailed can lead to a painful separation. Thinking about potential difficulties in advance mightn't be spontaneous and romantic, but could avoid unnecessary heartache.

Asymmetrical writing relationships

We have identified two dominant types of writing relationships where the imbalances of status, power and authority are significant. These are in the research team, and in the mentor–mentee relationship.

Writing with research teams

One of the most common complaints made by early career researchers is related to the way in which writing and publication is managed. Their concerns are numerous. Junior team members often suggest that they:

• are not given the opportunity to first author
• do the first draft and then are put last in the list of authors
• do the whole paper and then must wait months for senior colleagues to comment
• do the first to final drafts and then find senior colleagues, who have had no input, putting themselves as first author
• have their ideas presented as those of their senior colleagues
• find their first draft rewritten without consultation or discussion.

As well, junior team members may find that even when senior colleagues are involved, the work they produce is less than exemplary. They are then afraid to criticise their senior colleagues for their writing or argument.

The ideal answer to these kinds of problems is probably to choose a better team in which to be a junior member. Realistically of course, researchers don't always know how the team will work, and many young researchers are just pleased for the work. There is certainly an argument for better training for senior academics in managing and developing junior colleagues. At the very least, there is a strong argument for discussing and sorting out how authoring and publishing will be conducted at the start of each and every team project. The rules of engagement need to be specified.

There is an international agreement about who should be credited as an author. The Vancouver protocol (the protocol can be found on most university websites or in research handbooks) on authorship states:

> Authorship credit should be based only on substantial contributions to 1) conception and design, or analysis and interpretation of data; and to 2) drafting the article or revising it critically for important intellectual content; and on 3) final approval of the version to be published. Conditions 1, 2, and 3 must all be met. Participation solely in the acquisition of funding or the collection of data does not justify authorship. General supervision of the research group is not sufficient for authorship.

The Vancouver protocol does *not* deal with the question of which author should come first in the list, or who should take responsibility for what. Figure 8.1 shows one strategy Pat has used at the outset of research projects to create an explicit meeting agenda on publications.

While this kind of team discussion will not solve all writing problems that may arise, it is a good beginning and does focus attention on the fact that writing from a research project is potentially tricky. In the project referred to in Figure 8.1, this discussion led to decisions being recorded as a specific authoring protocol. We know that some universities are now developing authoring protocols and there are also in development a range of digital tools which offer statistical processes for determining the order of authors according to their contributions (see, for example, http://www.authorder.com).

A junior researcher, however, might take this idea of a research team discussion and/or a protocol or a tool to senior colleagues at the start of a research project, in order to initiate conversation about how the team will operate its publishing agenda. It should not simply be taken for granted.

Writing with mentors

Mentoring most often starts with supervisors during the doctorate, or with former supervisors immediately afterwards. It can of course, and often is, continued with more senior academics in formal mentoring schemes or in research project teams.

There has been research about the importance of mentoring to early career researchers keen to get on with publication.

There are several issues that we need to cover:

- Publications in research journals (and conference papers)
- Publications for a professional audience
- Publications that bridge professional and research audiences – i.e. a book
- Feedback to project stakeholders, local and national.

We need to do all this in a way that:

- is equitable, among members of the research team;
- is mutually supportive, and takes account of people's career needs;
- produces good work.

How would the writing be done, and who would do it?

We need first to decide on a principle: should all writing be done within the project? That is, should we say that any writing that uses data from the project should be discussed by the project team, and be cleared for publication by its directors? Having had experience from other projects about people 'going off with data' – quietly – I would say that the answer to this is 'yes'. This is an issue partly of quality control and partly of collegiality. BUT, I think that if there is disagreement about whether something should be published, it should be resolved – finally – in favour of the writer, with a disclaimer if necessary. Is this fair?

We should agree on – as a team of eight – the article topics. People should indicate a preference for topics on which they want to work, with Project Directors agreeing to the final allocation. Drafts should be circulated to all the team, and discussed by emails and where possible at team meetings.

We should make sure that everyone who wants to first author gets the opportunity to do so.

Figure 8.1 Excerpt from research project proposal about publications

Two international surveys by Dinham and Scott (2001) show a strong connection between publishing support and increased productivity. Encouragement from supervisors was an important aspect of proceeding to publication, with 'those participants who received this assistance more likely to publish than those who did not' (53). Page-Adams *et al.* (1995) report on a peer writing group of social work professionals who assisted each other to publish during candidature. Eight of the 25 doctoral students who joined the group submitted or published 19 papers during the group's first year, compared to only five papers produced by the 17 non-members. Their evaluation showed a positive correlation between group membership, scholarly output and the capacity to make a contribution to professional knowledge early in one's academic career. Lee and Boud's (2003) work with early career academics in an Australian university similarly demonstrated the significant impact of group mentoring on developing effective publication strategies. Participants were mid-career PhD students who held full-time positions at the university and were under pressure to develop a research profile. Their group meetings became rich sites for both fostering publications and doing what Lee and Boud call 'the making and remaking of academic identities' (189).

When Barbara investigated doctoral publication in the sciences and in education (Kamler, 2008), she found that early career science researchers expect as a matter of course that they will be mentored through co-authoring with supervisors.

> In general, the six graduates in science published more during the process of writing the PhD and aimed for more prestigious journals – in part, because their supervisors expected them to. Writing early in the research and co-authorship with supervisors were seen as standard and important tactics in preparing for post-doctoral work.
>
> (Kamler, 2008: 287)

While the six science graduates in her sample published 13 articles in international refereed publications – all of these co-authored with supervisors – the pattern for education graduates was starkly different. Only two of the six education graduates were successful in publishing in international journals. Significantly, however, these two articles were also the only two co-authored texts in the education sample. Why was there such a difference between science and education? Barbara suggests that it was the recognition in science of the importance of learning to speak in discipline-specific ways and the framing of this work as collaborative.

One of the education graduates who did co-author successfully described her supervisor's input in this way:

> I've really learnt from her . . . because anything I've written I've usually run past her. And she's given me feedback or at least said you might want to do a bit more reading here or a bit more thinking here or put it in and see what happens and then help me deal with the critique that's come back . . . In fact after my first go at writing a journal article, I probably would never have gone and done it again. I would have just thrown that one in the bin if I hadn't had that sort of assistance and feedback.
>
> (Kamler, 2008: 290)

These case studies confirm that co-authorship with supervisors was significant in getting a profile for doctoral researcher writing in *both* education and science. It was co-authorship that produced international refereed publication; without it, it did not occur. Co-authorship helped students move through the struggles and anxieties of publishing. It taught them how to be robust in the face of rejection and ongoing revision.

The benefits of co-authoring were also articulated by one of the most prolific writers in our interview sample, Michael Peters:

> Writing with Jim was a privilege because it was the best one-on-one that I could get. He was a trained philosopher and he was also reading very widely . . . He was reading Foucault and never ever made claims about what he'd read unless he'd actually read it. So I got to trust him and that trust was a really important element to it I think . . . But also a big motivator here was his opinion of me and what it felt like for me to have someone like Jim who was a professor at Auckland and I wasn't even faculty, you know, and he thought that I was good. And that kind of expectation – and that manifested itself in me being very directive in governing the kind of process.

Peters was aware that the impact on him as a novice was in part due to Marshall's status – he was well known and highly regarded – and Peters thus achieved ascribed status from the partnership. If the senior colleague was good and wanted to write with him, it meant he was good too. The partnership accomplished important identity work through writing as one voice.

But such partnerships are not always easy. Relationships between supervisors and their doctoral researchers are by their very nature asymmetrical in power and status. The often younger and certainly more junior partner may feel very vulnerable and exposed when working in a writing collaboration. Operating a first cut process for joint writing may in fact exacerbate such power differentials; if the doctoral researcher writes first they feel as if they are being marked when the supervisor takes over, and if the supervisor writes first, they may feel unable to contribute meaningfully to the draft text.

This power differential does not necessarily disappear when the doctoral student graduates. Science educator Stephen Ritchie is interested in collaboration in research teams (Ritchie, 2007b; Ritchie and Rigano, 2007). He has written about his own response to co-authoring with his former supervisor who subsequently became a research partner:

> I wrote the first draft. I felt a sense of frustration and disappointment with myself, however, when Michael returned the paper with the section on our dialectic-theoretical framework overwritten. Michael's additions clearly enhanced the paper, but this caused some initial anguish because I needed to reconceptualise my position on dialectics for the paper to progress further.
>
> (Ritchie, 2007a: 226)

Here we can see not only the problem of the junior scholar feeling somewhat inadequate, but also the difficulty of giving up a line of argument. This 'giving up' is always part of collaborative writing. Giving up may become very problematic in asymmetrical relationships where it can easily be assumed that it is the most experienced of the researchers whose version will be better, thus requiring the less experienced to make the adjustment. This, of course, is not automatically the case, but it can be tricky for a more junior colleague to persuade the more senior to change their mind and their text – especially so if it is a former supervisor!

Nevertheless, there are good reasons for experienced researchers to work with their students and more junior colleagues. To name just three: professing means supporting colleagues newer to scholarly pursuits; good succession planning depends on mentoring; and scholarly communities are built through collaborative work. What's not to like then about collaborative writing between senior and junior colleagues!

All of the writers we interviewed also discussed writing with students. They mentioned inter alia the need for academic generosity with students, passing on what they learned, and the care needed to build more overtly pedagogical relationships than those they enjoyed with their peers.

Many supervisors offer to co-author at least one refereed journal publication with each of their doctoral students. The first reason is to do with the importance of publication for career building; writing with a supervisor is a bit of a 'leg-up' in the field, as we have already seen. But there is a second and straightforward pedagogical reason, that writing together is hands-on learning about writing for publication per se. It's not talking about writing for publication as an idea – it's the reality.

Writing with doctoral students requires the supervisor to contribute knowledge about the genre as well as the debates and the field within which the writing is to find its niche. The doctoral researcher is more expert in the specific research project, and must not only contribute data, but also analysis and very often, particular theory. The journal argument is usually jointly developed in pre-writing conversations around the abstract, before the student writes the first draft; sometimes the supervisor writes the introduction which is then passed to the student to continue. This order of events seems to be quite common, but there are always issues about how much the supervisor writes over the doctoral work.

Mindful of the kinds of responses that can arise from asymmetries of authority and status, such as those expressed by Ritchie above, supervisors often feel reticent about imposing too much of their own version of events on the actual text. Pat, for example, always puts herself as second author on co-written texts. This has generally been a good strategy, although it proved problematic on one occasion when very critical referee comments required a much stronger theorisation to be applied to a resubmitted article. The doctoral student was unable to do this and so Pat had to write this in, altering the argument but leaving the empirical example as developed through doctoral research. This theory–empirical divide did, unfortunately, reinforce the inequities of knowledge within the writing collaboration.

Writing with doctoral and/or early career researchers need not, however, be a dull and one-sided process. Kathryn Herr says that working with doctoral researchers is often highly pleasurable:

> We started from what seemed to me to be unrelated interests and got to the place where we saw how they were linked. So that was fun. I think, for me, when a collaboration really stretches me in terms of my thinking that's what I would call the fun of it, compared to where you are kind of slugging along and thinking: are we there yet?

Even though mentoring relationships are by their nature less equal than those between peers, and there is a greater need for scaffolding and for clear guidelines about who does what, there should be mutual benefit. In our view, the point of mentoring is not simply to support the mentee to become more independent and expert, although that is crucial, it is also to provide mentors themselves with space and time to learn, grow and take pleasure in new partnerships.

So what, now what?

The scholars that we interviewed were clear about the ways in which being mentored, writing together and mentoring others were integral to their development as scholars. From their conversations we have identified three different approaches and four key characteristics of productive writing relationships. We have also canvassed the problems that can occur and stressed how important it is to specify the rules of engagement before the writing begins.

We now want to return to text work/identity work and in the final chapter of our book, consider how the production of texts can be strategically developed for the individual emerging scholar. Our focus is on the peer reviewed journal article as a building block to a scholarly working life.

Chapter 9

Living hand to mouse

Engaging in dialogue with our chosen discourse community/ies means that writing for peer reviewed publication is an ongoing and career-long task. Writing a single article and getting it published is an achievement, but sustained writing is a hallmark of academic life; it is the way in which we engage with our peers close and distant, present and future. So one contribution to a scholarly conversation is just that – one contribution. In this final chapter, therefore, we want to address the question of writing with purpose and intent in and for the longer-term.

It is not difficult to see publication and building a career as somewhat serendipitous, something of a lottery. At a time when more people than ever have doctorates, when there appear to be less funds available for work, and when some pesky baby boomers stay working because they/we enjoy what they/we are doing, academic jobs are harder to get. Competition for post-doctorate scholarships is fierce, and the alternatives within higher education are either a teaching position, where it is difficult to find time for research and writing, or working as a research fellow, where there is time to do other people's research and writing but first authorship is difficult to achieve. Jobs outside the academy have the additional challenges of keeping connected with a library, and thus up to date with the literatures, as well as maintaining academic networks. However, despite all these difficulties, which we do not want to underestimate, there is still opportunity for taking some control. There *are* ways to minimise the risks and maximise the choices and chances that may occur. One crucial step in taking charge of the risky scholarly career trajectory is through ongoing publication.

To conclude our book, we offer three key strategies that support the development of a writing agenda. They are key, we think, to building a coherent and significant contribution to knowledge via text work/identity work. The three strategies are: developing a publication plan; building support for writing through finding writing mates and writing groups; and becoming a reviewer.

We start with publication planning. We begin by outlining some of the key principles of publication planning and then examine two variants which are useful at different career stages.

What is a publication plan?

A publication plan allows the writer to think strategically about the kinds of writing that are necessary to build a career and become known in one or more chosen fields. It covers a range of publication genres – conference papers, book reviews, special issues, edited books, monographs, professional publications and social media – as well as the associated key readerships/discourse communities. A publication plan offers a mechanism for pre-determining a range of outputs from research, from doctorates to large-team projects. It is also a timetable for writing based on a realistic appraisal of what is possible. As such, a publication plan allows the researcher to think about what resources they might need in order to accomplish the writing they want to do: study leave, a fellowship, a little more project funding.

A publication plan requires imagination. In order to think about what kinds of publications might be developed over a medium term, the writer has to consider the kinds of contribution that they wish to be known for. This has then to be conceived as an agenda – one which is ambitious and deliberately designed to profile the writer in particular scholarly conversations.

A publication plan is a working document. It is not intended to be printed and bound and put on a shelf. It is a file which is added to and modified as opportunities come along, and as new possibilities emerge from working with colleagues or from engaging over time with research data. It is often thus both a digital file and a piece of paper kept in a conspicuous place in the writer's working space.

Key pointers for building a publication plan

We offer four principles which underpin any publication plan. We have put these in bold to emphasise their importance.

It is helpful to **begin a publication plan before the PhD is completed**. This not only allows the researcher to begin to build a scholarly CV, but to develop an important competence – the capacity to see how to break up a large text and/or project into a set of smaller articles. We have often referred in this book to the problem with writers trying to cram all of their doctorate into one article. One strategy to avoid this is the publication plan. The researcher takes a metaphorical carving knife to the large slab of matter that constitutes the project or the thesis, and turns it into a series of discrete items. This requires devising a set of 'angles' on the material and imagining how these might become separate arguments, each of which makes a distinct and distinctive contribution. Doctoral research projects typically lend themselves to two or three articles from the findings, but there might also be a further paper in the methodology and another derived from the literature work. Some researchers find that they are able to write a scholarly monograph, while others have the basis for an innovative territory-marking special issue or edited collection.

It is helpful to **think ahead about which conferences to go to and what papers to present**. Conferences are a good way to test out a set of ideas, to build networks from interested audiences, and to 'dry run' an argument. However, there are also traps in conferences. We see many people whose CVs are littered with conference papers which they fail to turn into articles: this is because their goal has simply been to write the paper. It has not been written with a journal and a discourse community in mind. Another way to say this is: It has been written for the layer 2 of the conference and requires an enormous amount of work to get it right for the layer 2/3 practices of the journal. It is for this reason that we say the publication plan must always connect the conference with the target journal to which the paper will be sent. Our maxim is: write the journal article first, then present it at a conference – not write the conference paper, then convert it to an article later.

The other trap we often see is when people choose one or two conferences that they like and then never attend any others. While this means that they can become known within a particular discourse community, they can also become cosily bogged. They never risk going outside of their safe space to test out their contribution in the wider community and this crisis of imagination is ultimately career-limiting. It is important, we think, to use the process of publication planning not simply to establish and consolidate a place, but also to extend and stretch what it is we can do and say.

Similarly, it is important to **think beyond a small number of familiar journals**. Some fields support a wider array of specialist and generalist journals than others. But it is career-helpful for specialist researchers to not only build their profile within their specialisation, but also to explore how their knowledge might make a contribution to the field more generally, and to other specialist areas. Some disciplines, of course, have a discrete number of journals which are arranged in a hierarchy, and the goal in such fields is to work through all of them, and ultimately to publish in the most prestigious.

We know that some readers might expect us to say that it is crucial to publish in the most prestigious journals and to aim for these at the start. But what are the most prestigious journals? There is a great deal of debate about the kinds of calculations used to rank journals, not to mention the benefits of open versus closed publication and the commercial rapacity of particular journal publishers. There are conflicting opinions about whether doctoral and early career researchers should aim first off to publish in the journals that are highly ranked in indices such as the Thomson Reuters Social Science Index and Sciverse Scopus.

It is unusual, in our experience, for writers new to their discourse communities to write with the levels of authority required in the 'top' journals. However, some will be able to do this. So there is no hard and fast rule about whether to aim at the outset for the most difficult or something relatively possible. Each writer must assess their ambitions, their capacities to cope with critique and their understanding of their own field in order to develop their plan. And, as with the single article, mentors and other brokers can help talk through this process. In our view, which we re-state here, the goal of the early career researcher is to build a publishing profile, not to get one article in print.

We think it is important to **consider various types of publications** – professional, scholarly and those generated for engaging the public in the work that we do. Each of these different readerships expect and respond to different kinds of texts. Each of these different kinds of texts requires practice. It is no easier to write a column for a monthly magazine than to write a scholarly paper: each has a particular genre, register and lexicon that needs to be understood and mastered in order to meet the expectations of readers. These days it is important for scholars to be able to work across these genres as well as to use a range of social media to communicate their research and to engage in conversation with interested others. The publication plan therefore needs to allow for the traditional conference paper and refereed journal article as well as these other kinds of writing outlets.

We now consider the two variants of publication plans that we work with. The first is for those still engaged in doctoral research, while the second is for those a little way beyond the doctorate.

(1) Doctoral publication planning

When Barbara works with recently graduated doctoral students to create a publication plan, she suggests they use the following set of headings:

Title:
Abstract:
Target journal:
Back up journal (if rejected):
Related conference:
Time line for: writing the draft, delivering the conference paper, interacting with first readers, submitting the journal article

The starting point is to imagine four separate articles and write four separate abstracts after researching appropriate target journals for each. This involves getting knowledgeable about the discourse community, their goals, and editorship practices, much as we outlined in Chapter 2. But the labour involved in finding the angle and argument – and asserting the contribution for peers (rather than examiners) – should not be underestimated. It is hard work to divide and dissect a text the writer has spent so many years putting together.

Some years ago, Barbara worked with a junior colleague who produced a publication plan of nine articles – each corresponding to the nine chapters of her thesis. Such a neat correspondence is rarely doable; it cuts the data and argument too thinly. In this case the writer needed to learn how to borrow material across chapters – data, methodology, background – in order to mount a coherent argument for each article. Writing and rewriting her abstracts and brokering discussions with a mentor resulted in five articles, rather than nine.

In our experience, the earlier the planning process can begin, the better. Ruben, a medical anthropologist, made critical decisions about how to structure his thesis, based on his assessment of future publication possibilities. His research was a case study of men diagnosed with cancer, interacting with the internet and their medical practitioners. He was urged by his supervisor and colleagues to adopt a common anthropological format, with chapters organised around each of his five case-study male participants. But Ruben decided early on that this would make publishing later on very difficult. Journals did not want case studies. Instead, he opted to sort his findings chapters around key themes: masculinity and illness; medicine and new technologies; cancer and general medicine practices. He could then imagine a wide array of journal articles, each related to these themes, where he could mount a number of arguments using research data from across the case studies.

This facilitated a strategic approach to publishing. In fact, Ruben produced three articles and won a post-doc the year after he completed. But it is worth noting that not everyone approved of his strategy. He was viewed by some in his department as ruthlessly career-oriented and superficial for eschewing in-depth case-study writing. This was in 2003; perhaps he was ahead of his time, perhaps not. But by ignoring the conventions of his university culture, he successfully built a career and a publication profile at the same time. Considerable identity work and text work indeed!

Many doctoral graduates, however, do not begin publication planning until after the thesis is completed, submitted and passed. The example of Jessie, one of Barbara's PhD students, suggests this can be a more difficult option. Jessie's thesis was a narrative study of migrant women's experiences with the law in Australia. She developed an interdisciplinary approach using scholarship from critical race theory, feminist legal theory and narrative methodologies. Her overall argument was that, despite successful legal outcomes for the women, they remained highly distressed by their treatment and the often invisible racist and discriminatory practices in the community.

The thesis was well written. But the skilful way Jessie crafted the stories of the eight women and the eight legal and welfare professionals who interpreted the women's stories made it extremely difficult for her to carve up the text. In fact, her first publication plan described four articles for four journals, but as Jessie herself said during her first brokering discussion, 'These all sound the same, don't they?' They had different titles and a slightly different nuance, but offered the same condensation of the whole thesis, its methodology and overall findings. There was no So what, no specificity, no Locating or understanding of the various journal discourse communities.

It took many months and many iterations of the publication plan until it became a workable document. A key move was learning to understand the conversations in the journals so Jessie could join in, rather than pronounce in general terms what she found. She could then cut her data and use her different disciplinary lens with greater focus and specificity. So for example, for the *Australian Feminist Legal Journal* she eventually used only one woman's story of racial discrimination, but emphasised the responses of the legal and welfare practitioners in order to explore unnamed discrimination in the professions; for *Qualitative Studies in Education* she focused on the tiered narrative model she developed, in which the women's first-hand accounts are compared with those told of the same event by welfare and legal professionals; for the *Journal of Intercultural Studies*, she focused only on workplace violence. Her multiply revised abstract (see Abstract 9.1) for this latter journal illustrates the greater focus, direction and So what she finally achieved.

Violence at work: narratives of race and gender in professional life

Whilst information relating to research on workplace violence has outlined its high financial cost, together with the physical and psychological forms it assumes, little is known about the causes or contexts of workplace violence. Issues relating to the race, gender and class of the individuals concerned have been notably missing from these accounts. This article aims to extend our understandings of workplace violence experienced by CALD (Culturally and Linguistically Diverse) women. It uses the narrative methods of critical race theory to present the stories of two black African women, working in professional jobs in Australia. Their accounts describe the context and forms of the violence they experienced, its effects on their personal and working lives, and the different legal means used to confront it. Their stories underline, not only the pervasive, covert and systemic nature of race discrimination in the Australian workplace, but its personal and institutional costs, together with the uses and limitations of legal forms of redress.

Abstract 9.1 Jessie finds her argument through publication planning

The point we draw from Jessie's experience is that publication planning can be as complex as writing the thesis. And it can be facilitated by conversations with a publication broker. However, doctoral students who make and revise publication plans get much better at 'not saying everything' and developing the kind of focus the editors in Chapter 3 say they want. Writing the first article can be excruciating. But it is much easier when the writer knows what the three or four other articles will do. They can then rest assured that, even though they are cutting out what they feel is crucial material, it will be covered elsewhere.

(2) Early career publication planning

Early career researchers are likely to be juggling more than one piece of research. There may still be work to be extracted from the PhD itself, as well as new work that has begun. It is important to have a way of thinking about this old and new work that allows the researcher to feel that they are in control of the agenda, rather than always chasing deadlines and never finding the time to actually follow anything much through to completion.

We see a very recognisable syndrome in our early career workshops. This is where the researcher has produced a number of conference papers – however these have never been worked on again. Researchers tell us that they don't have time to do this. They feel bad, guilty even, certainly inadequate. Yet the production of conference papers seems also to show them that they are somehow engaged in scholarship, albeit of a half-done variety. They are clear that conference paper production without final publication is problematic, and yet they still keep submitting more abstracts and producing more and more incomplete papers. The production of serial conference papers is a little like a car stuck in the sand, the wheels are revving, but there is no movement forward!

Some institutions have now moved to prevent this kind of repetitive activity and only give conference funding to people who convert the conference paper to the finished article. But the big stick approach assumes that early career researchers don't want to move on, *and* that they know how to make this shift. We think that big sticks are counter-productive unless they are accompanied by some serious support.

We offer the research-conference-publication schedule as one piece of scaffolding that might be helpful in effecting the shift from serial conference paper to a publication agenda. We offer a timetabling approach (Table 9.1) that requires researchers to think about the process of getting from research to publication. This involves analysing the desired publication outputs, the outlets and the venue in which the output will be tested.

There is only one rule that applies in this process and this is: **Never write a conference paper. Always write a draft of the article that will be submitted**. This means that the target journal must be considered at the time that the publications are being planned, rather than the conference. Conferences are then chosen on the basis of which will provide the best site for potentially useful feedback *prior* to the final refining of the paper.

In Table 9.1 we show a sample publication plan, using some of Pat's schedule of research for 2012. The major thing to note is the headings on the columns. These start with the *research* and then go on in order to the kinds of *planned publications* that will emanate from it. While not all of these can be anticipated, some can, and because this is a living document, more can always be added and if necessary some removed and/or changed. The next column is the *outlet* – the target journal or book chapter. This is followed by the *title and abstract*, again a working document that can be hyperlinked to this master text. The penultimate column is the *conference* venue. Of course not all articles and chapters have to be tested out and so this might be a column which is not filled in for every output.

The last column is the *timeline*. This is very important and must be taken seriously. It is critical to make time for writing. Prolific writers all make time to write. Take Stephen Ball for instance, who notes the importance of not simply expecting time to be there and feeling regretful when it's not. He makes sure he is:

> cutting out segments of time well in advance. Actually going through my diary and drawing in it with a highlighter, putting borders around days or mornings, and then rigorously keeping to that. Because if you don't write them in, if you're looking for spaces next week or even next month, you're probably too late. So, what I used to do at the beginning of each term was to make sure there was some time every week to write . . . it's a discipline in terms of organizing time. You have to sit down and just organize your time, to ensure there are spaces for writing. To give it the priority it deserves.
>
> (Carnell *et al.*, 2008: 72)

Table 9.1 Sample timetable for research and publication

RESEARCH PROJECT	OUTPUTS: PLANNED PUBLICATIONS	OUTLET: TARGET JOURNAL (shortlist of journals identified but not yet specific journal)	TITLE and ABSTRACT (hyperlinked to actual abstract)	TESTED OUT: CONFERENCE	TIMELINES Due dates for abstract, submission, expected publication
Royal Shakespeare Company	Two journal articles	Drama Education	TITLE		
		Teacher Professional Learning	TITLE	AERA	
	Chapter in arts education book		TITLE		
Ethnographic observation of artists	Three journal articles	Early Childhood	TITLE	AARE	
		Vocational Education	TITLE		
		Research Methodologies	TITLE		
	Website				
	Chapter in arts in education book				
Impact of community theatre	Working papers				
	Website				
	Journal article	Community development	TITLE	BSA	

We agree. It's very important – no, it's critical – to carve out the space to write, and to do this in relation to the writing tasks that need to be accomplished.

Using some kind of scheduling is the only way to avoid getting caught up in multiple deadlines which all occur at the same time. This is likely to happen anyway due to the sheer pragmatics of teaching, bidding for funding, not to mention life in general, but it is vital to plan for this not to happen. Having some kind of timeline for writing means that we can see the consequences of spontaneous decisions to do something additional, and then do the necessary adjustments to our planning. This kind of publication planning also supports applications for study leave and for life. When do we need to ensure that there is a spare weekend rather than one or two hours each morning? How can we take advantage of term break to give the writing a boost? When do our funders need to see some publications emerging? These are all questions that can be considered through a timetabling approach.

Of course, like dieting, sticking to a publication plan is not necessarily easy. Many people find that its much easier if they have some support from others engaged in the same process.

Writing with first readers

Support groups are helpful. However they are insufficient in and of themselves. Any support group needs shared activity. We suggest that this support activity ought not only to be about sharing frustrations, targets, successes and disappointments, but also focus on the group members' writing as well. Interacting early with first readers can help shape and craft our texts as well as keep us on track with our writing plans.

When we show our work to a trustworthy support network we do not have to wonder: Is this clear? Does the reader get what I want them to? Does this bit work? What more do I need to put in here to make the point? We can interact with trusted colleagues, friends and others who are willing to engage with our texts while they are still in formation, before they go to the wider public. Working with a writing mate can provide this kind of support, as can working in a writing group. We offer an example of each from Pat and Barbara's experiences of facilitating 'first reader' communities.

Writing mates

Pat teaches a doctoral writing course in her university. She suggests that doctoral researchers work with at least one, sometimes two or three, writing mates. These are people who meet regularly, say once a month, just like a reading group, to share writing-in-progress. Pat suggests that doctoral writers always start by talking about the writing that they are trying to do, the audience and purpose. She provides writing mates with a feedback template that they can use for the first few meetings to give each other feedback.

The template (Figure 9.1) focuses primarily on what the writer has actually done, rather than on what they haven't, and on whether they have communicated what they intend. Only after this has been determined does the conversation move to some suggestions for improvement.

The summary is a key aspect of this activity. Articulating a summary first allows the writer to assess whether their argument is clear. Following this with strengths allows the writer to understand that the critique that follows doesn't mean that they should give up because the piece is hopeless. They have something to work with, even if it's not yet ready.

This kind of first reading is a safe way to begin to engage with the scholarly practice of critique. It provides a venue in which doctoral researchers can share writing experiences and help each other as peers to develop their writing, using feedback they have received. Writing mates report back periodically during course time about what and how they are doing.

Writing groups

Barbara runs writing groups for universities interested in building their institutional writing cultures. There are a variety of ways to run these groups to ensure ongoing interaction with first readers (see, for example, Aitchison, 2003, 2009, 2010; Aitchison and Lee, 2006; Cuthbert and Spark, 2008; Lee and Boud, 2003). A common thread is a group commitment to refine writing before it is sent out for review.

Barbara suggests that writing groups meet regularly, approximately every four to six weeks, and that a roster is drawn up at the start so everyone knows exactly the date when they will present their draft. This minimises the impulse to opt out due to workload or anxiety. She also suggests that groups have an appointed leader. The person does not have to lead discussion, but oversees the administrative details – a system for circulating drafts, reminders about the

---

Tell the writer your summary of the argument in this writing.

Tell the writer what you think the point is that they are trying to make.

Name two strengths of the writing.

Say what you think is the most important thing for the writer to do in order to improve it – this must not be secretarial, that is, not about spelling, grammar or sentences.

Figure 9.1 Writing mates: template for giving feedback

next meeting, booking a regular meeting time and space – to ensure the smooth running of the group.

Writing groups are potentially vulnerable hot spots. Writers get nervous about showing imperfect writing-in-formation to a public, even a friendly one. We are so used to reading polished text that the mess of a draft can cause embarrassment, unless there is a skilled method for reading. The aim here is *not* to repair the paper or hunt for errors, but to get inside the writer's argument and help them achieve their goals for a specific readership. The group operates, in a sense, as a rehearsal for the journal review process, working together to make the text work better. For this reason, Barbara likes to formalise the rules of reading and engagement at the beginning of a group. We show these in Figure 9.2.

Principles

1. All members of the writing group make a serious commitment to reading and responding to the papers for every meeting. The concept requires an ongoing serious commitment as both a reader and writer by all group members.
2. Group members respect the intellectual work of writers, our colleagues, and in our practice maintain a clear distinction between the individual and their written work to which we are responding.
3. Meetings and interactions adopt a democratic and safe procedure that builds trust and support to achieve the primary aim of the group – to share and develop our work collaboratively to foster journal publication.

Procedure

1. For each writing group meeting, draft papers from two writers will be distributed to all members of the group, one week prior to the meeting so members have sufficient time to read.
2. Draft papers should be sufficiently developed so they provide readers with a coherent structure, idea and argument, at the level of a complete draft.
3. The writer always speaks first. Discussion begins with the writer making a brief statement about the key argument, intended journal and audience. They indicate key struggles or features of the writing they are worried about. This sets the context for the discussion and reminds readers they are not the only ones who see problems in the text.
4. Group members respond by first saying something positive – what works well, pinpointing particular sections or ideas or structuring or phrasing they like. Only then does discussion move to what does not work and how the text might be improved. The most useful kind of feedback to writers is specific, rather then vague or general. We do not focus on proofreading and corrections. It is too early.
5. The writing group meeting usually last for two hours, with approximately 45 minutes devoted to each paper and some additional time for reflection and planning for the next meeting. An alternate version is a one-hour meeting that considers only one paper.

Figure 9.2 Writing-for-publication group principles and procedures

Writing groups create spaces for being generous and critical. Discussion is frank but not negative. People don't just say nice things for fear of hurting the writer, but they also don't go for the jugular. In the process members learn to be more robust in receiving critical feedback (good preparation for the real review process, discussed in Chapter 7) and get to know their colleagues' work in a way that does not always happen in busy institutions. As one group member said:

> It is one of the few forums where we're invited to be intellectually rigorous and it's okay to actually engage across the table in a bit of cut and thrust. 'I don't understand this idea. Please explain, clarify, help me understand'. Whereas in most other forums where we meet, there is this level of politeness and compliance when we present our points of views. There is nowhere else in the faculty where we get this kind of interaction. You need it.
>
> (Personal communication)

Both writing mates and writing groups offer the kind of support that should not be optional. Like supervisor mentoring, they provide a scaffold and safety net. They can provide the kind of support that many of us need in order to build and maintain a scholarly career. They are sociable as well as intellectually stimulating and this is always important for sustaining motivation and energy.

In conclusion to this chapter and this book, we discuss a final move to make in relation to building a publishing agenda. It is a step which goes into the heart of the discourse community and which gives a different insight on the publication process.

Getting inside: reviewing and learning to review

One final strategy to make clear how scholarly publication works is to get closer to the process. The first step towards this is to become a reviewer for one or more journals.

There are multiple ways in which one can become a reviewer. Supervisors can involve their doctoral students in the reviewing that they do. University graduate schools can sponsor postgraduate journals run by students for students. Academics can support students to take on the various roles, referee, editor, proofreader and so on, while a first publication outlet is provided at the same time. There are some journals which always have students as first reviewers. They do the job of deciding whether articles should be sent out to review or not. There are also entire journals run by students – the *Harvard Education Review* is one.

Early career researchers can put themselves forward as referees for journals. They might also decide to submit a proposal for a special issue to a journal. Special issues are a good way to put one's own writing in the same volume as more experienced and better-known academics. Editing a special issue builds networks and readers and lays down a marker in the field. However, the editing experience is a rich site for scholarly knowledge production in its own right. An analysis of the experiences of three early career researchers who edited a special issue shows that:

> they engaged in philosophical work, through writing an editorial and choosing books for review; market work, through negotiations with the publisher; profile work, through the activities that enhanced their own scholarly careers, networks and identities; relational work, through working with each other, with referees and with authors; textual work, through selection of articles and giving feedback to authors; and secretarial work, through the process of refereeing and production.
>
> (Thomson *et al.*, 2010: 147)

In these kinds of editing and reviewing sites, it is important for early career writers and researchers to receive clear guidance about the ethics of reviewing. In his book, *Academic writing and publishing: A practical handbook*, Hartley (2008) signals dissatisfaction with what might be called ungenerous reviewing practices and urges reviewers to:

- Be courteous throughout. There is no need to be superior, sarcastic or to show off. Remember the paper you are refereeing might have been written by a postgraduate, and it could be a first attempt at publication.
- Avoid criticising the paper because it does not do what you might have done. Judge it on its own merits.
- Explain any criticisms that you make. There must always be a reason for them.

(Hartley, 2008: 154–155)

Very few journals offer such explicit advice to reviewers. Some, however, do. Figure 9.3 shows guidelines issued to referees by the *International Journal of Learning*.

Doctoral researchers may need more support than this. Some explicit scaffolding from a mentor, for reading the article and writing a review, is particularly useful.

> ### Role of the Referee
> Referees are requested to observe the following guidelines:
> - **Expertise:** Papers are not always sent to a referee whose field is identical to the subject matter of that paper. You don't have to be precisely qualified in a field to be a constructive referee. In fact, an excellent paper will speak beyond its narrowly defined field. If, however, a paper is so distant from your field that you do not feel qualified to judge its merits, please return it to the publishing manager for the journal, who will locate another referee.
> - **Confidentiality:** Referees receive unpublished work, which must be treated as confidential until published. They should destroy all electronic and printed copies of the draft paper and referee report once they have received confirmation that their reports have been received by the publishing manager (in case we can't open the report files you send us). Referees must not disclose to others which papers they have refereed; nor are they to share those papers with any other person.
> - **Conflict of Interest:** Referees must declare any conflict of interest or any other factor which may affect their independence—in cases for instance, where they have received a paper of a colleague or an intellectual opponent. In cases of conflict of interest, please notify the publishing manager of your inability to referee a particular paper.
> - **Intellectual Merit:** A paper must be judged on its intellectual merits alone. Personal criticism or criticism based solely on the political or social views of the referee, is not acceptable.
> - **Full Explanation:** Critical or negative judgments must be fully supported by detailed reference to evidence from the paper under review or other relevant sources.
> - **Plagiarism and Copyright:** If a referee considers that a paper may contain plagiarism or that it might breach another party's copyright, they should notify the publishing manager for the journal, providing the relevant citations to support their claim.

Figure 9.3 Instructions to reviewers

When it comes to reading the article, we recommend taking an appreciative, critical stance, rather than one dominated by the will to offer a killer critique. We have all heard many horror stories about shocking reviews – including most recently a writer who was given a mark out of ten by a reviewer (Mary Helen, personal communication) – and it's important to remember those when reading. We are not reading with the goal of finding every possible side angle and reference that *could* be made. Rather, the task is to see what the writer's intentions are, how they have staged their argument, whether they have achieved what they set out to do and what kind of contribution this makes.

A useful strategy is to read the abstract and the article right through once. The goal is to see what the author is trying to say and to grasp the paper as a whole text. Next, read the abstract and article again asking the ten questions outlined in Figure 9.4.

(1)   Does the paper fit in the journal? Does it address an issue/problem/report on a piece of research which the readers of this journal will find relevant and/or of interest? The answer here is likely to be yes, since editors usually weed out articles that don't fit before they send them out, but it's useful to ask the question.

(2)   What is it about the paper that will be of interest to readers of this journal? What existing debates, spaces in the literature, problems or issues does it address? Is it connected to ongoing conversations in the journal, and if so how? Does it explicitly refer to other articles in the journal about the same topic? What does it offer that is new? (Remember it just needs to be new enough and important enough to this readership, not world shattering.)

(3)   Does it establish a clear warrant for its topic within current policy/practice or the field, and if not, is the lack of warrant a problem in this journal – that is, are all articles expected to be explicitly situated in the field of readers' interest in some way? The vast majority of journals expect this.

(4)   Does it have a point to make? Does it have one, or at most two, ideas – or is it hard to work out what the point is? Could the point be made clearer, and if so where and how – check the introduction for a statement of intent and the conclusion. Can you summarise the point the article is trying to make in a sentence or two? If you can't do this, then there is a problem with the article.

(5)   Does it refer economically to the key literatures and/or theoretical resources it needs in order to make its case? Or does it offer an inappropriate peacock's display of reading?

(6)   If it is an empirical piece of work, do you know enough about how the research was conducted to trust it? Do you understand the basis on which the writer says they will make claims? If it is a theoretical piece, is there sufficient detail about the theory to allow you to follow the way it is used? Or is it a set of quotes strung together?

(7)   If it is an empirical piece of work, is this reported in a way that is comprehensible and defensible? Does it go beyond the merely descriptive to offer some kind of interesting analysis? Is there enough evidence to show how the analysis has been made? Does this seem robust and rigorous? If quantitative, are the calculations accurate and sound? If qualitative, do the interpretations seem well justified?

(8)   Does the conclusion address the 'So what? Who cares?' question? What difference does it make, to whom and why? Or is it just a restatement of the article? Is the abstract a fair representation of the article that you've read? Does the title aptly sum up the essence of the piece? If you found this title online would you want to click on it to go further?

(9)   Is the article well written? Is the prose too dense or too naïve? Is it well balanced, that is, not top- or back-heavy? Are there enough headings or too many? Could you understand the argument in the article just from reading these headings? Are the sections in a logical order or does the reader get lost? Is there clear signposting for readers to follow, particularly if the argument is complex?

(10)   Does the article meet the journal conventions in titling, headings, referencing and word length? Does the English expression need attention? Has the article been carefully proofread?

Figure 9.4 Questions to guide reading an article to be reviewed

The answer to these questions will provide sufficient information to make a decision about whether the article is publishable, needs revisions and if so, to what extent, or whether it should be rejected.

When it comes to writing the review, a good maxim to is to write the kind of comments we would like to receive. While most journals suggest that feedback to authors should be positive and offer concrete advice, this does not always happen.

Clearly it is important not to be rude, sarcastic or patronising, but it is just as important to be clear and specific. If there is a problem, say what it is and don't waffle. Don't say: 'The references need attention'. Say: 'The references need to be in the appropriate journal style'. Don't say: 'The methodology section needs work'. Say: 'The methodology section needs to include information about the site, sample and types of data generated as well as the method of analysis'.

Figure 9.5 presents a framework Pat has developed for giving clear feedback to authors. She devised this in response to a query from an early career researcher who was worried about what to do with his first review. It continues to be the section of her blog (http://patthomson.wordpress.com) that receives the most visits, which probably indicates the dearth of discussion there is about how to avoid being the demon reviewer.

Generally she aims for three quarters to a page in length but stresses this is ONE way, not the only way, to approach the task.

Writing reviews can be very eye-opening. The process not only helps us to understand what reviewers are looking for and how we might respond to the comments that we receive on our published papers, but also helps us think more generally about the whole writing-for-publication process. In thinking through the criteria we might apply to review others people's work, we can also think how we might use those same criteria when we next write. We can even take note of strategies used in the papers we review – the kinds of rhetorical moves that are used, for example, to establish the niche, the ways in which the discourse community interests are met, the words that are used to signal the writer's authority.

These insights are very helpful to all writers as they work their way through writing their own articles and books.

Signing off

Our intention, when beginning this book, was to write something that would complement the kinds of advice that were already on offer in other texts and online. We set out to establish a theoretically grounded approach which would attend to both text work/identity work, layers 1, 2, and 3 and writing for

(1) Write two to four sentences summarising what the paper is about, as in: *This paper addresses . . . and presents evidence that . . . The author/s argue that . . .* This gives the author the chance to see whether you have understood what they wanted to say. If you haven't got it, they can then consider how they might have produced this misreading.

(2) If you really enjoyed reading the article, say so before you start with the concerns.

(3) Write something about the contribution, as in: *The article clearly makes a contribution to/has the potential to add to what we know about/will make a significant addition to . . .* This might be linked to a caveat such as . . . *but needs further work in order to bring this to fruition/realise its potential, needs some revision in order to achieve this.*

(4) Then, if there are suggested revisions, say whether they are major or minor and how many there are, as in: *I have two suggestions for major revisions and one more minor point . . .* or *I offer some issues that the author/s needs to consider in the methodological section and a recommendation for some restructuring of the findings . . .*

(5) Then dispassionately state the changes that you think are necessary, based on your reading of the article. Try to focus on the things that are the most fundamental.

(6) You may just outline the problem(s) and suggest that the author needs to find a way of resolving it/them. You might offer one or two suggestions. Or you might have something very definite in mind. If you are suggesting major revisions, then there isn't much point in outlining twenty-five specific things for the author/s to do; it's the big bits that are the most important for the author/s to grasp. Too much detail and they will be completely confused/overwhelmed/dispirited. If there is reading that the author/s need to do, give them the references, don't just say there is literature out there that they ought to know about.

(7) Finally, succinctly list any grammatical, proofing and referencing problems.

(8) Conclude with some encouragement. This might involve repeating the potential contribution and the importance/value of the author/s continuing to work on the piece.

Figure 9.5 Pat's rules for writing referee reports

specific discourse communities. We also wanted to provide a range of useful strategies which could be adopted and adapted by individuals and groups. We think we've achieved what we set out to do. We wonder whether readers agree.

To that end, we are always interested in what people do with our work. We invite readers to contact us to tell us about their journal writing experiences. Barbara can be contacted via her website http://www.writingdesigns. com.au/ and Pat can be contacted via her blog http://www.patthomson. wordpress.com or on Twitter @ThomsonPat.

References

Aitchison, C. (2003). 'Thesis writing circles'. *Hong Kong Journal of Applied Linguistics, 8*(2), 97–115.

Aitchison, C. (2009). 'Writing groups for doctoral education'. *Studies in Higher Education, 34*(8), 905–916.

Aitchison, C. (2010). 'Learning together to publish: Writing group pedagogies for doctoral publishing'. In C. Aitchison, B. Kamler and A. Lee (Eds.), *Publishing pedagogies for the doctorate and beyond* (83–100). London: Routledge.

Aitchison, C., and Lee, A. (2006). 'Research writing: Problems and pedagogies'. *Teaching in Higher Education, 11*(3), 265–278.

Anderson, G., Herr, K., and Nihlen, A. S. (2008). *Studying your own school: An educator's guide to qualitative practitioner research* (2nd ed.). Thousand Oaks, CA: Corwin Press.

Appiah, K. A. (2005). *The ethics of identity.* Princeton, NJ: Princeton University Press.

Baert, P., and Shipman, A. (2005). 'University under siege?' *European Societies, 7*(1), 157–185.

Bauman, Z. (2004). *Identity.* Cambridge: Polity.

Becker, H. (1986). *Writing for social scientists: How to start and finish your thesis.* Chicago, IL: University of Chicago Press.

Becker, H. (undated). Some words about writing. *Writing across boundaries,* http://www.dur.ac.uk/writingacrossboundaries/writing/howardbecker/ (Accessed 3 December 2011).

Belcher, W. L. (2009). *Writing your journal article in 12 weeks: A guide to academic publishing success.* Thousand Oaks, CA: Sage.

Bjork, L., and Raisanen, C. (2010). *Academic writing: A university writing course.* Lund, Sweden: Studentlitteratur.

Boice, R. (1990). *Professors as writers: A self-help guide to productive writing.* Stillwater, OK: New Forums.

Bourdieu, P. (1990). *In other words: Essays towards a reflexive sociology.* Stanford, CA: Stanford University Press.

Braidotti, R. (2011). *Nomadic subjects: Embodiment and sexual difference in contemporary feminist theory* (2nd ed.). New York: Columbia University Press.

Bruner, J. (1986). 'Life as narrative'. *Social Research, 54*(1), 11–32.

Canagarajah, A. S. (2002). *A geopolitics of academic writing.* Pittsburgh, PA: University of Pittsburgh Press.

Carnell, E., MacDonald, J., McCallum, B., and Scott, M. (2008). *Passion and politics: Academics reflect on writing for publication.* London: Institute of Education.

Casanave, C. P., and Vandrick, S. (Eds.). (2003). *Writing for scholarly publication: Behind the scenes in language education.* Mahwah, NJ: Lawrence Erlbaum.

Culler, J., and Lamb, K. (Eds.). (2003). *Just being difficult? Academic writing in the public arena.* Stanford, CA: Stanford University Press.

Cuthbert, D., and Spark, C. (2008). 'Getting a GRIP: Examining the outcomes of a pilot program to support graduate students in writing for publication'. *Studies in Higher Education, 33*(1), 77–88.

De Lange, T. (2011, September). *Writing an article based thesis: Experiences from a Norwegian context.* Paper presented at the European Conference for Educational Research, Berlin.

de Lauretis, T. (1987). *Technologies of gender: Essays on theory, film and fiction.* Bloomington, IN: Indiana University Press.

Deane, M., and O'Neill, P. (2011). *Writing in the disciplines.* Basingstoke: Palgrave Macmillan.

Delanty, G. (2001). 'The university in the knowledge age'. *Organization, 8*(2), 149–153.

Dinham, S., and Scott, C. (2001). 'The experience of disseminating the results of doctoral research'. *Journal of Further and Higher Education, 25*(1), 45–55.

Du Gay, P., Evans, J., and Redman, P. (Eds.). (2000). *Identity: A reader.* London: Sage.

Dunant, S. (1994). *The war of the words: The political correctness debate.* London: Virago.

Dunleavy, P. (2003). *Authoring a PhD: How to plan, draft, write and finish a doctoral dissertation or thesis.* London: Palgrave.

Elbow, P. (1973). *Writing without teachers.* New York: Oxford University Press.

Epstein, D., Kenway, J., and Boden, R. (2005). *Writing for publication.* London: Sage.

Fairclough, N. (1989). *Language and power* (1994 ed.). Singapore: Longman.

Fairclough, N. (1992). *Discourse and social change.* London: Polity.

Fairclough, N. (1995). *Media discourse.* London: Edward Arnold.

Fairclough, N. (2003). *Analysing discourse: Textual analysis for social research.* London: Routledge.

Fine, M., and Weis, L. (1998). *The unknown city: The lives of poor and working class young adults.* Boston, MA: Beacon Press.

Fine, M., and Weis, L. (2000). *Speed bumps: A student friendly guide to qualitative research.* New York: Teachers College Press.

Fine, M., and Weis, L. (2003). *Silenced voices and extraordinary conversation: Reimagining schools.* New York: Teachers College Press.

Fish, S. (1980). *Is there a text in this class? The authority of interpretive communities.* Cambridge, MA: Harvard University Press.

Fortanet, I. (2008). 'Evaluative language in peer review referee reports'. *Journal of English for Academic Purposes, 7*(1), 27–37.

Foucault, M. (1978). *The history of sexuality: An introduction* (R. Hurley, Trans.). New York: Pantheon Books.

Game, A., and Metcalfe, A. (1996). *Passionate sociology.* London: Sage Publications.

Graf, G., and Birkenstein, C. (2010). *They say, I say: The moves that matter in academic writing* (2nd ed.). New York: W. W. Norton & Co.

Griffiths, M. (1998). *Educational research for social justice: Getting off the fence.* Buckingham: Open University Press.

Hacking, I. (2006). 'Making up people'. *London Review of Books, 28*(16), 23–26.

Hartley, J. (2008). *Academic writing and publishing: A practical handbook.* London: Routledge.

Herr, K., and Anderson, G. (2005). *The action research dissertation: A guide for students and faculty.* Thousand Oaks, CA: Sage.

Holmwood, J. (2011). *A manfesto for the public university.* London: Bloomsbury Academic.

Ivanic, R. (1998). *Writing and identity: The discoursal construction of identity in academic writing*. Amsterdam: John Benjamins.

John-Steiner, V. (2000). *Creative collaboration*. New York: Oxford University Press.

Jonsson, S. (2006). 'On academic writing'. *European Business Review, 18*(6), 479–490.

Kamler, B. (2008). 'Rethinking doctoral publication processes: Writing from and beyond the doctorate'. *Studies in Higher Education, 33*(3), 283–294.

Kamler, B. (2010). 'Revise and resubmit: The role of publication brokers'. In C. Aitchison, B. Kamler and A. Lee (Eds.), *Publishing pedagogies for the doctorate and beyond* (64–82). London: Routledge.

Kamler, B. and Thomson, P. (2004). 'Driven to abstraction: Doctoral supervision and writing pedagogies'. *Teaching in Higher Education, 9*(2), 195–210.

Kamler, B., and Thomson, P. (2006). *Helping doctoral students write: Pedagogies for supervision*. London: Routledge.

Kamler, B., and Thomson, P. (2007). 'Rethinking doctoral work as text work and identity work'. In B. Somekh and T. Schwandt (Eds.), *Knowledge production: Research in interesting times* (166–179). London: Routledge.

Kamler, B., and Thomson, P. (2008). 'The failure of dissertation advice books: Towards alternative pedagogies for doctoral writing'. *Educational Researcher, 37*(8), 507–518.

Kellaway, K. (2011). 'The 10 best love stories'. *The Observer,* http://www.guardian.co.uk'culture/gallery/2011/feb/2013/ten-best-love-stories-in-pictures (Accessed 13 June 2011).

Lavie, J. (2006). 'Academic discourses on school-based teacher collabaration: Revisiting the arguments'. *Education Administration Quarterly, 42*(5), 773–805.

Lee, A. (2010). 'When the article is the dissertation: Pedagogies for a PhD by publication'. In C. Aitchison, B. Kamler and A. Lee (Eds.), *Publishing pedagogies for the doctorate and beyond* (12–29). London: Routledge.

Lee, A., and Boud, D. (2003). 'Writing groups, change and academic identity: Research development as local practice'. *Studies in Higher Education, 28*(2), 187–200.

Lee, A., and Kamler, B. (2008). 'Bringing pedagogy to doctoral publishing'. *Teaching in Higher Education, 13*(5), 511–523.

Lillis, T., and Curry, M. J. (2006). 'Professional academic writing by multilingual scholars: Interactions with literacy brokers in the production of English-medium texts'. *Written Communication, 23*(1), 3–35.

Lillis, T., and Curry, M. J. (2010). *Academic writing in a global context: The politics and practices of publishing in English*. London: Routledge.

McAlpine, L., and Akerlind, G. (2010). *Becoming an academic: International perspectives*. Basingstoke: Palgrave Macmillan.

McDowell, L. (2004). 'Work, workfare, work/life balance and an ethic of care'. *Progress in Human Geography, 28*(2), 145–163.

MacIntyre, A. (1984). *After virtue: A study in moral theory* (2nd ed.). Notre Dame: University of Notre Dame Press.

Malloy, C. J., Moscowitz, T., and Vissing-Jorgenson, A. (2009). 'Long-run stockholder consumption risk and asset returns'. *The Journal of Finance, 64*(6), 2427–2479.

Mills, C. W. (1999). *The sociological imagination*. Buckingham: Open University Press.

Murray, R. (2005). *Writing for academic journals*. Buckingham: Open University Press.

National Advisory Committee on Creative and Cultural Education (NACCCE). (1999). *All our futures: Creativity, culture and education*. London: HMSO.

Nygaard, L. P. (2008). *Writing for scholars: A practical guide to making sense and being heard*. Oslo: Universitetsforlaget.

Osberg, D., and Biesta, G. (2010). 'The ends of education: Complexity and the conundrum of inclusive educational curriculum'. *International Journal of Inclusive Education, 14*(6), 593–607.

Page-Adams, D., Cheng, L. C., Gogineni, A., and Shen, C. Y. (1995). 'Establishing a group to encourage writing for publication among doctoral students'. *Journal of Social Work Education, 31*(3), 402–407.

Paré, A. (2010). 'Slow the presses: Concerns about premature publication'. In C. Aitchison, B. Kamler and A. Lee (Eds.), *Publishing pedagogies for the doctorate and beyond* (30–46). London: Routledge.

Peters, M., and Besley, T. (2007). *Subjectivity and truth: Foucault, education and the culture of the self.* New York: Peter Lang.

Peters, M., Marginson, S., and Murphy, P. (2008). *Creativity and the global knowledge economy.* New York: Peter Lang.

Peters, M., and Marshall, J. (1999). *Wittgenstein, philosophy, postmodernism, pedagogy.* Westport, CT: Bergin & Garvey.

Petre, M., and Rugg, G. (2011). *The unwritten rules of PhD research* (2nd ed.). New York: McGraw Hill, Open University Press.

Pole, C. (2007). 'Researching children and fashion: An embodied ethnography'. *Childhood, 14*(1), 67–84.

Power, M. (1997). *The audit society: Rituals of verification.* Oxford: Oxford University Press.

Power, M. (2004). *The risk management of everything: Rethinking the politics of uncertainty.* London: Demos.

Readings, B. (1996). *The university in ruins.* Cambridge, MA: Harvard University Press.

Reid, N. (2010). *Getting published in international journals: Writing strategies for European social scientists.* Oslo: Nova.

Ritchie, S. (2007a). 'Success in research collaborations'. In S. Ritchie (Ed.), *Research collaboration: Relationships and praxis* (225–235). Rotterdam: Sense.

Ritchie, S. (Ed.). (2007b). *Research collaboration: Relationships and praxis.* Rotterdam: Sense.

Ritchie, S., and Rigano, D. (2007). 'Solidarity through collaborative research'. *International Journal of Qualitative Studies in Education, 13*(1), 129–150.

Rivzi, F., and Lingard, B. (2009). *Globalising education policy.* London: Routledge.

Rolfe, G. (2009). 'Writing up and writing as: Rediscovering nursing scholarship'. *Nurse Education Today, 29*, 816–820.

Rose, M. (2009). *Writer's block: The cognitive dimension.* Carbondale, IL: Southern Illinois University Press.

Rottier, B., Ripmeester, N., and Bush, A. (2011). 'Separated by a common translation? How the British and the Dutch communicate'. *Pediatric Pulmonology, 46*, 409–411.

Soler, V. (2007). 'Writing titles in science: An exploratory study'. *Journal of English for Academic Purposes, 2*(4), 327–341.

Strathern, M. (Ed.). (2000). *Audit cultures: Anthropological studies in accountability, ethics and the academy.* London and New York: Routledge.

Sullivan, P. (undated). *Writing with your head in your hands,* www.dur.ac.uk/writingacrossboundaries/writingonwriting/patricksullivan/ (Accessed 10 February 2010).

Swales, J. (1990). *Genre analysis: English in academic and research settings.* Cambridge: Cambridge University Press.

Swales, J., and Feak, C. (1994). *Academic writing for graduate students: Essential tasks and skills.* Ann Arbor, MI: University of Michigan Press.

Swales, J., and Feak, C. (2004). *Academic writing for graduate students: Essential tasks and skills* (2nd ed.). Ann Arbor, MI: University of Michigan Press.

Swales, J., and Feak, C. (2009). *Abstracts and the writing of abstracts*. Ann Arbor, MI: University of Michigan Press.

Sword, H. (2012) *Stylish academic writing*. Cambridge, MA: Harvard University Press.

Taylor, C. (1989). *Sources of the self: The making of modern identity*. Cambridge: Cambridge University Press.

Taylor, S., Rivzi, F., Lingard, B., and Henry, M. (1997). *Educational policy and the politics of change*. London: Routledge.

Thomson, P. (2010). 'Headteacher autonomy: A sketch of Bourdieuian field analysis of position and practice'. *Critical Studies in Education, 51*(1), 1–16.

Thomson, P. (2011). 'Creative leadership: A new category or more of the same?' *Journal of Educational Administration and History, 43*(4), 249–272.

Thomson, P., Byrom, T., Robinson, C., and Russell, L. (2010). 'Learning about journal publication: The pedagogies of editing a "special issue"'. In C. Aitchison, B. Kamler and A. Lee (Eds.), *Publishing pedagogies for the doctorate and beyond* (137–155). London: Routledge.

Thomson, P., and Gunter, H. (2008). 'Researching bullying with students: A lens on everyday life in a reforming high school'. *International Journal of Inclusive Education, 12*(2), 185–200.

Thomson, P., and Kamler, B. (2010). 'It's been said before but we'll say it again: Research is writing'. In P. Thomson and M. Walker (Eds.), *The Routledge doctoral students' companion: Getting to grips with researh in Education and the Social Sciences* (149–160). London: Routledge.

Thomson, P., and Walker, M. (2010). 'Last words: Why doctoral study?' In P. Thomson and M. Walker (Eds.), *The Routledge doctoral students' companion: Getting to grips with research in Education and the Social Sciences* (390–404). London: Routledge.

Vincent, K. (2012). *Schoolgirl pregnancy, motherhood and education: Dealing with difference*. Stoke on Trent: Trentham Books.

Wagner, J. (1993). 'Ignorance in educational research: Or, how can you not know that?' *Educational Researcher, 22*(5), 15–23.

Wellington, J. (2003). *Getting published: A guide for lecturers and researchers*. London: RoutledgeFalmer.

Yates, L. (2004). *What does good educational research look like?* Buckingham: Open University Press.

Index